It is possible to be a Christian, to hold the full, orthodox, biblical faith, and yet reject a view of the Bible that sets it over against science and reason. It is possible to believe that the Bible is the inspired Word of God, from start to finish, and yet reject ideas of biblical infallibility over matters of history and cosmology. It is possible because it is the way its human authors and its divine Author intended . . . It is not just possible. It is a positively enriching thing to be released from a narrow, literalist view of the Bible to see it as it is, a dynamic Word, speaking as eloquently to modern man in his technology as it did to ancient man in his tents.

Believing the Bible

by
David Winter

Morehouse-Barlow Co., Inc.
Wilton, Connecticut 06897

ISBN 0-8192-1325-X

First edition published 1980
Hodder and Stoughton Ltd.
Mill Road
Dunton Green
Sevenoaks, Kent
England TN13 2YA

First U.S. edition published 1983
Morehouse-Barlow Co., Inc.
78 Danbury Road
Wilton, Connecticut 06897

Library of Congress Catalog Card Number 82-62582

Printed in the United States of America

CONTENTS

BUT THIS I *CAN* BELIEVE

Can an intelligent person believe that the Bible is true? That seems to be a stupid question, because many obviously intelligent people do believe it, and make no secret of the fact. Yet my experience over recent years has convinced me that many intelligent people, in other respects very sympathetic towards Christianity, in the end turn their backs on it because they believe that Christian faith involves accepting the literal truth of all of the Bible, and that is something they simply cannot bring themselves to do. I have talked with scores of people in that situation, and something of a pattern emerges. Many of them would like to believe and many of them used to believe, when they were children. But as they have grown up and learnt more, so they have come to discard belief in an historically infallible Bible as a relic from an earlier, more gullible age. And with that belief they have also discarded belief in Jesus Christ.

I remember an interview with a young student in Loughborough. He had been brought up in a strict evangelical home, where the literal truth of the Bible was never questioned. He had learnt the great Bible stories at his mother's knee—Adam and Eve, Noah, Samson, David and Goliath, John the Baptist and, of course, Jesus, the Son of

God. No distinction was made between the credibility of Noah and Jesus. One simply accepted them all as essential parts of the one faith.

What he had been given, he explained, was a 'package'. Salvation depended on trusting Jesus as your Saviour, but that in turn depended on the total reliability of the Bible, God's Word. If one were to cast doubt on the reliability of the Bible in any single respect—say, Balaam's talking ass— then assurance of salvation was jeopardised. After all, if one could not rely on what the Bible told you about the ass, how could you rely on what it told you about Jesus?

So, along with repentance, faith and baptism went a whole conglomeration of other things which had to be believed: creation in six days, a literal garden of Eden, a universal flood and a prophet who travelled in the belly of a great fish. To deny any of these was tantamount to a denial of the faith. Eventually this young man passed his 'A' levels and went on to university to study science. Somewhere along the way the doubts and misgivings began to clarify. Could it possibly be that the Bible his parents revered and set their lives by was a less than reliable guide in matters of history, biology and physics? Was it after all possible that the facts, as he found them in his studies, flatly contradicted some of the things the Bible said? And was evolution—a theory equated with the antichrist at home—perhaps the guiding principle of life on this planet?

Eventually there came the moment he and his parents had dreaded, when the tension between the 'facts' of science and the 'facts' of the Bible reached breaking point. He decided that his parents were wrong. The Bible, and hence Christianity, was disproved. From that moment on he would be an unbeliever.

He was not, however, a happy unbeliever. He had not rejected Christianity because it failed to meet his deepest

8

human needs, or because its moral demands were unacceptable. It was, for him, a starkly simple issue. He had been told, over and over again, that to attempt to reconcile science and the Bible was inconsistent with true faith—indeed, it was an evil compromise. There was, for him, no middle ground, no other way of looking at the Bible: his parents and his church had seen to that. He could not be persuaded that the important point was not that his parents were wrong about science, but that they were wrong about the *Bible*. He could not see that it might be possible to believe in Jesus Christ and all the great Christian doctrines without being tied to the cosmology of Genesis or the historicity of Noah's ark.

He was the victim of a closed system and closed minds, but the biggest tragedy of all is that the view of the Bible he had once accepted, and now rejected, is a travesty of the truth. He had thrown away his Christianity for nothing—to solve a non-existent contradiction, an illusion of incompatibility. And there are many like him.

This book is written for them. It is not the first, of course. There has been no shortage of books aimed at the erstwhile but troubled orthodox Christian. But most, if not all of them, and certainly the most widely read, like those by Don Cupitt and Hubert Richards, have taken a radical view of the Bible and an unorthodox view of the Christian faith.

This book is for troubled orthodox Christians who want to remain orthodox. It is a belated attempt, by someone who has been through the experience himself, to save others from unnecessary inner conflict and turmoil. It *is* possible to be a Christian, to hold the full, orthodox, biblical faith, and yet reject a view of the Bible that sets it over against science and reason, as though irrationality and credulity were the hallmarks of faith. It *is* possible to believe that the Bible is the inspired Word of God—from start to finish—and yet

9

reject ideas of biblical infallibility over matters of history or science. It is possible because it is the correct way to read it, the way its human authors and its divine Author intended.

Indeed, it is not only possible. It is a positively enriching thing to be released from a narrow, literalist view of the Bible to see it as it is, a dynamic Word, speaking as eloquently to modern man in his technology as it did to ancient man in his tents.

1: DID JONAH SWALLOW THE WHALE?

Many years ago, when I was a student, a missionary speaker came to give a talk to our church youth fellowship. I cannot remember anything of what he had to say, nor (I fear) even his name, but I do recall that his use of the Bible worried me. I was fresh from a vivid experience of personal conversion, the reality of which remains with me to this day, but nevertheless I could not ignore his heavy-handed literalism. When it came to question-time, I asked him whether he believed that everything in the Bible was literally and factually true. Although the occasion is every bit of twenty-five years ago, I can give his reply verbatim. 'If the Word of God said Jonah swallowed the whale, I'd believe it.'

He got a good, appreciative laugh from his audience, and went quickly on to the next question. In that moment, I knew that I could never be a fundamentalist.

Of course many Christians would say that they believe the Bible to be 'true' from cover to cover—some adding 'including the maps'. There is a certain kudos to be gained in some circles from such statements, and anyone who questions them is regarded as at best a 'compromiser' or at worst a traitor. For many there is a kind of perverse security in loudly proclaiming their faith in the impossible, and the more incredible the object of their belief the greater their apparent security. Yet I believe this 'security' is a thing of straw, because it is not based either on fact or reason. Merely asserting that something is so does not actually make it so, and the fact is (and I use the word 'fact' carefully) that nobody who really gives the matter ten minutes serious thought could argue that the whole Bible is factually or historically true.

One sentence will do, from Psalm 19, where we are told quite categorically that a tent is fixed in the sky for the sun. Does anyone today believe that that is factually true? But if it is not, then the 'whole' Bible is not factually true and the point is conceded that sometimes the Bible expresses true *ideas* in non-factual or poetic ways. Indeed, I shall try to show that a good deal of the Bible speaks in this way, and we miss its full impact if we insist on taking it literally.

Now if the whole Bible—Genesis to Revelation—is not to be taken as literally or factually true, the question is raised which I have set myself to answer in this book: what *are* we to believe about the Bible? If it is not possible simply to accept all of it in a wooden and literalistic way (and I have to say that hardly anybody does, in practice), then how are we to accept it? We do not live, as our forefathers did, in a world where the boundaries between poetry and fact were blurred; nor do we live, as the writers of the Bible did, in a world where 'history' and 'story' were virtually synonymous, rather than opposites. It is hard to persuade modern people that the most profound truths of all are better and more truthfully told in poetry and story rather than in the devalued coinage of allegedly factual reporting and its analysis; or that the Bible's truth as often falls into the first as the second category.

So we have an agreed conspiracy in many churches. The preacher, who has probably spent many years studying the Bible and its background, is aware of the truth of what I have just written, but he is anxious not to disturb his 'simple lay-people'. For their part, the 'simple lay-people'—who are not at all 'simple' when it comes to assessing politicians or the relative value of a 7·3 per cent wage claim—do not wish to be disturbed by having to rethink their attitude towards the source-book of their faith. Consequently, week in and week out, the preacher simply avoids the difficulty. In effect, he uses the Bible not as the Word of God (which, by definition, would be a living thing) but as a kind of celestial Old Moore's Almanack. He confines himself to minute textual exposition—and gets a thoroughly undeserved reputation for being 'deep'; or he uses biblical texts simply to decorate or validate homilies on various aspects of Christian truth, without troubling to put those texts into their context, nor concerning himself with any wider questions about them than whether they serve his immediate purpose.

I have said that the 'simple lay-people' are part of this conspiracy, but that is not wholly true. Many, many ordinary Christians are utterly perplexed by the situation. Far from being partners to a conspiracy of silence they are tortured by a painful awareness of the gulf between what they hear from the pulpit and what they know—from their wider reading, or from their own studies in history, science or theology—to be true. They have no desire at all to abandon their Christian faith, which they know from their own experience to be valid and authentic. They are not looking for a 'way out' from Christian commitment, nor for some softer option than the full, orthodox Christian faith demands. And they see, many of them, that the alternatives to a belief in the inspiration of the Bible are unattractive and ineffective. Yet the tension remains. Should they, because it seems to 'work' for others, silence the insistent voice of reason and endorse the verbal infallibility of the Bible? Or is there some way in which they can retain a workable doctrine of biblical inspiration without denying their God-given rationality?

Now these are not just academic questions, though you might think so from reading most of the books on the subject of biblical interpretation. For those of us whose faith depends on the reliability of God's revelation to man, this can never be simply a matter for intellectual conjecture, with theories and concepts bandied about, to be accepted or rejected according to the prevailing flavour of scholarly opinion. As Fr Anthony Parish, a Jesuit scholar, has pointed out, the 'pendulum of critical opinion never stands still but continues to swing from one critical consensus to another'. It is not at all unusual to find one 'expert' embracing in his academic career three or four different theories about, say, the nature of the Gospels, each, in its day, held to represent the consensus of scholarly opinion, each, after its day, rejected as inadequate. Some of us, faced with this, are tempted to say that theology is too serious a subject to leave to the theologians.

This book is not a contribution to a theological debate, but an attempt to work out a credible, authentic and honest approach to the Bible which will enable people like me to accept it as the Word of God without being committed to a package deal of doctrines about infallibility and verbal inspiration which comparatively modern controversies have attached to it. If such an approach cannot be found, then the choice before the orthodox Christian is appalling—either a bloodless liberalism, which virtually invites the believer to write his own creed, or a blind fundamentalism, which flourishes in the twilight world of fanaticism and superstition, and repels many sensitive and intelligent people who are looking for faith.

DID JONAH SWALLOW THE WHALE?

Of course, most Christians have not gone to either extreme: not because they have worked out a better theology, but because they do not like what they see there. The conspiracy of silence is largely the work of people who intuitively reject those extremes, but have been unable or unwilling to work out an approach to the Bible which avoids them.

For me, this came to a head over a radio programme which I produced for the BBC at Christmas 1978. It was called 'Bethlehem—what really happened?' and was an attempt to evaluate the historical content of the traditional nativity narratives.

When the programme was first proposed, I must admit I saw it as an opportunity to re-examine these well-known and often sentimentalised stories and re-assert their basic historicity. I cannot say that I had ever studied them very closely, and I was vaguely aware that there were difficulties in harmonising the accounts by Matthew and Luke; but I assumed that conservative scholars had faced these and that the narrative of events connected with the incarnation of Christ could be shown to be essentially historical.

I invited Philip Crowe to write and present the programme. I knew him as an evangelical clergyman who had for seven years taught New Testament at a conservative Anglican college. I also knew—an essential qualification for this programme—that he was a man of quite devastating honesty, who would take the programme seriously and pursue the questions it raised ruthlessly to a conclusion.

And that was how it turned out. It was a programme of almost painful honesty, serious and even ruthless in its treatment of the subject, and disturbing both to those who made it and many of those who heard it.

What I discovered as I worked on it was that I had for years ignored the problems raised by the nativity stories because, deep down, I was afraid of facing them. As we talked to biblical scholars—conservative and radical, Catholic and Protestant—a whole new picture emerged, a new way of looking at the Bethlehem story. I shall go into this in more detail later in the book, but I found the experience, while traumatic, profoundly encouraging. I emerged from it with my belief in the inspiration of the Bible strengthened, even though I was now looking at Matthew's account of the visit of the Wise Men (for example) in a poetic and allegorical way rather than as a piece of rather dubious history.

It was then that I decided that I should try to write this book, for people like myself. It is not the work of a biblical scholar or a theologian, but of someone who has spent his working life—as a teacher, a journalist and a radio producer—trying to communicate the Christian faith to modern people, and who has discovered, rather late in the day, that the whole question of how we handle the Bible (hermeneutics, to give it its technical name) is the key to doing it effectively. To go back to my opening story, I cannot believe that God would ask me to accept that Jonah swallowed the whale, because that would be to deny the rationality of the world he has created.

But that God has spoken, through history, through people, through events, through story and poetry, and that this perfect revelation of himself and of ultimate truth is to be found in the Bible . . . this I *can* believe.

2: OBJECTIONS

Before trying to set out an approach to the Bible which avoids the extremes of scepticism and superstition, I should like to look at some of the objections readers might make to the whole exercise. Many of these objections were to be found in the first hundred or so of the letters we received about our 'Bethlehem' programme. Others have been expressed, often forcefully, when this subject has been debated openly. And yet others, from the opposite extreme, are evoked by any attempt to modify the consensus of radical theological opinion.

Undoubtedly the objection which I feel most strongly is that which alleges that to raise doubts in people's minds about the accuracy of the Bible is in fact to raise doubts in their minds about its *authority*. The argument goes something like this: As most Christians are quite content to accept the literal truth of the Bible, and as the most successful sections of the church are those where this is most uncritically accepted, why question it? Is not this simply 'doing the devil's work'—undermining simple faith, instead of reinforcing it? This view can often be heard in both evangelical and Roman Catholic quarters.

As an objection, it has to assume that the person who is

17

questioning the traditional interpretation of the Bible is doing so irresponsibly. It takes for granted that there is a clear and equal choice between 'reinforcing' simple faith and 'undermining' it, and that the questioner has opted for the latter rather than the former. It also assumes that his motives are suspect—the possibility that it is his *conscience* that drives him to do it is more or less excluded. And finally it suggests that he should preach and teach biblical infallibility even though he is convinced it is an erroneous view of Scripture.

In fact, of course, few people actually prefer doubt to faith. Certainly I get no satisfaction at all out of 'undermining' anyone's faith, including my own, and given the choice I would sooner settle for an assured, dogmatic Christianity than one full of doubts and questions. Certainty has an enormous appeal; uncertainty is a debilitating thing.

But that is not the choice. The choice is between a dogmatic Christianity which inflexibly demands what many people cannot intelligently give, and a Christianity which tries to meet the seeker and the doubter where they are. Now if meeting them in this way involved abandoning the biblical Gospel, it would indeed be a futile exercise, for there would be nothing of substance left to offer them. But if, as I shall argue, it actually involves interpreting the Bible *as its original writers intended*, it is an exercise in which all believers ought to join enthusiastically.

Sooner or later, any intelligent youngster brought up in a traditional Church is going to have to face the problems raised by modern biblical and historical studies. Sadly, many are unprepared for it, and when confronted with what looks like irrefutable evidence that what they have been taught, and believed, is simply not so, they relapse into unbelief. Others, of course, silence their doubts, and enter on to a lifetime of spiritual schizophrenia, divorcing 'faith'

18

from 'facts' and relegating their religious beliefs to some private mental cupboard isolated from the real world and their rational approach to it. I believe that this phenomenon may well explain the otherwise inexplicable contradiction between belief and behaviour (especially over things like business practices, money and sex) which is sadly common in fundamentalist circles.

Others—and especially those with some theological training—respond to the challenge of biblical scholarship with a different schizophrenia. They accept the 'liberal' view privately, but for a variety of motives maintain the 'conservative' view in public, or at any rate use 'conservative' language. Sometimes this is because they fear they will lose a treasured job, perhaps in a Bible college or popular pulpit. Sometimes this is because they have accepted the argument that it is their vocation to strengthen rather than disturb faith. And sometimes it is because they cannot face the upset, hurt and anger which they fear would inevitably follow if they were to preach what they really believed. I can certainly say that the average evangelical or Roman Catholic layman would be astonished, and deeply shocked, if he knew what many of his pastors and teachers really believed about the Bible.

But what concerns me is not the anger and shock which the traditionalist feels, but the gulf that this situation creates between many sensitive and intelligent people and the orthodox Christian faith. What is a bulwark of faith to some is a barrier to faith for others, and it is not good enough for Christian pastors and teachers to opt out of this dilemma by placating (and, I believe, patronising) their 'simple lay-people' at the expense of the genuinely perplexed, the genuinely seeking and the genuinely doubting. There must be a way, and it must be found, to meet the needs of both groups.

Another reaction to the challenge of biblical criticism could be summed up in the advice, 'Tell the story'. This school of thought—very widespread in the 'main-stream' churches[1]—argues that biblical interpretation is too complex, and the opinions about it too contradictory, to make it a practical option in a pastoral and teaching ministry. So— it is suggested—the Church simply 'tells the story', in Word and sacrament, and the believers are nourished by it at different levels. Some will take it literally, at face value, and be re-assured. Some will receive it poetically or allegorically, and it will speak to them in its own way. Some will respond to it as to a myth (in its proper sense), a story which communicates a truth though it is not itself true.

I can see the attraction of this argument, for at a stroke it removes many of the most painful decisions facing the Christian communicator. It has a kind of intellectual respectability about it, and it can be given a spiritual element which removes it completely from the sphere of human debate and argument—we 'leave it to the Holy Spirit'. He is the only reliable interpreter of Scripture and he will see that each member of the Church is nourished by it according to his needs.

Nevertheless, I think this is a spurious approach. Obviously it is true that the Holy Spirit is both the originator and the interpreter of Scripture, but simply to 'tell the story' is to imply that we do not know at all what it means. Where, then, is any doctrine of a 'teaching Church'? Where is the value of a ministry of the Word? Is not this to turn the Church into a shrine where unexplained rituals and strange stories are told, for all the world like some eastern mystical cult? Is not this the death of Christianity as a religion rooted

[1] The Report 'Evangelism in England Today' to the General Synod of the Church of England (1979) actually uses the word 'Story' (with a capital 'S') throughout as a synonym for the Gospel.

in real history, genuinely incarnate and related to actual people in time and space? Painful though it may be, I am sure that we must not only 'tell' the story, but interpret, explain and apply it in the terms within which it was originally given.

One conservative evangelical writer of the last decade has addressed himself extensively to this problem, Dr Francis Schaeffer, and there is no doubt that some younger evangelicals have found his approach re-assuring. They have made their way in their thousands, mostly from the colleges of North America and Western Europe, to his 'hide-out' in the Swiss Alps, looking for an answer to the conflict between a revealed religion (within which most of them have been brought up) and the pressures of modern philosophy and science. Schaeffer himself has described vividly the kind of young person who turns to him for help—intelligent, sensitive, often artistic, and rebelling against an ugly and often insensitive fundamentalism.

Schaeffer's answer is to set the Christian revelation very firmly in time and space, and then to demonstrate that it is the only 'universal' to make sense of all the 'particulars' of knowledge which they bring with them. Music, art, science, history, anthropology, mechanics—he has little difficulty in demonstrating that they are a nonsense unless related to some all-embracing universal which gives them meaning and rationality. The alternative, he argues, is to conclude that existence itself is a nonsense.

So far, so good. But the weakness in Schaeffer's approach, so far as the problem of the Bible is concerned, is that he insists that the revelation of God must be expressed only in space-time historical events. So he argues for a literal Garden of Eden, a literal Adam and Eve, a literal temptation and Fall, a literal tower of Babel, and so on. Here, it seems to me, he has become the slave of his own philosophy, and is forcing the Bible into a mould for which it was not designed.

I once asked him, in connection with his literal interpretation of the opening chapters of Genesis, whether he believed that poetry could 'tell the truth' as truthfully as history. 'Not in this case,' was his answer. For him, the Fall has to be historical, or nothing. It seemed to me then, and does even more forcibly now, that to put an intelligent person in the position where he must choose between a blanket acceptance of a literal (and to me, erroneous) interpretation of a passage of the Bible, on the one hand, or total unbelief, on the other, is quite monstrous. For that reason, I believe, Francis Schaeffer failed to meet the needs of those whose problems were about the Bible, rather than philosophy. Sadly, while accurately diagnosing the problem, the solution he offered was little more than a circular argument—the Bible is literally true because my theory demands that the Bible be literally true.

It may be that among those young people who flock to L'Abri (as Schaeffer called his mountain centre) there is a budding theologian who will be able to re-express Schaeffer's insights into truth and reality on the basis of a less rigid and unimaginative approach to the Bible. If that were to happen, then a genuinely Christian philosophy might emerge in the modern world.

What seems certain is that the opposite extreme to Schaeffer—biblical radicalism—has even less to offer the ordinary Christian. This approach to the Bible, which has arisen as a logical response to the arguments of one of this century's greatest New Testament scholars, Rudolph Bultmann, virtually removes Christianity from any historical basis. It says that there is practically nothing that we can know for sure about the historical Jesus, and so what we have in the New Testament are the attempts of his earliest followers to express in words and stories the impact his life had made on them. Consequently, for the modern reader there is little more than a shadowy portrait of a man who reflected reality and ultimate truth in his life. All we can do, then, is to respond to that vision or ideal, hoping ourselves to receive something of what the first Christians experienced through the re-telling of the story of Jesus.

The resurrection, for instance, 'cannot be demonstrated or made plausible as an objectively ascertainable fact on the basis of which we can believe'. It can, Bultmann asserts, only be believed 'in so far as the risen Christ is present in the proclaiming word'—that is, as the Gospel is *experienced*.

The radical theologians of today follow on from that position. Some of them would echo Bultmann's claim that the quest for an historical Jesus is irrelevant to the faith of Christians, and would direct us instead to the faith which the 'Jesus event' created in others, and which we can experience today. Others reject his extreme scepticism about the historical value of the Gospels, and have embarked on a new quest to discover an historical 'core' in the New Testament, though without offering anything remotely like certainty concerning either the words or the actions of Christ.

But this, it seems to me, is a 'Gospel' without any authority. Individuals who have thought it through have, it is true, sometimes had their faith renewed, as though they had somehow 'plugged in' to the authentic spirit of Christ. But it seems an esoteric, abstract kind of spiritual experience, which bears little relation to the authority and dynamic of the Christian Gospel as traditionally proclaimed. To put it more concretely, I cannot recall ever having met a single person who was converted from unbelief to Christianity by the radical Gospel.

Not only that, but this approach does not seem to do

justice to the Bible itself. It is, at best, at one extreme end of the pendulum swing of critical opinion, and treats the historical content of the Gospels in a cavalier fashion. Once again, it seems to be an instance of a theory shaping biblical interpretation, rather than *vice versa*.

So we are left with the question with which we began. Can there be found an answer to the problem of the interpretation of the Bible which is reasonable, credible and positive, and which retains both the authority and the converting power of the Gospels?

3: THE GOOD SAMARITAN: TRUE OR FALSE?

'A certain man went down from Jerusalem to Jericho.' So begins one of the best-known parables of Jesus, the story of the Good Samaritan.

But *did* a 'certain man' go down to Jericho? Is this an historical account of an actual event? There is no indication in the narrative that this is to be taken as anything other than a straight-forward historical account, used by its narrator to make a moral and ethical point. If this passage were taken at face-value, apart from our wider understanding of Jesus's teaching methods, there would be no reason at all for doubting that it was intended to relate a matter of historical fact.

As it happens, we have all decided that it is a 'parable'— 'an earthly story with a heavenly meaning'. There may have been a 'certain man' to whom these events occurred. On the other hand, there may not. We do not regard it as important. Indeed, although I must have heard scores of sermons on this story, I have never heard a preacher even raise the question of its historicity. The value and meaning of this passage simply does not depend upon its historical truth, but on a powerful moral idea expressed in a vivid, human story.

Now it is not very difficult to decide that the story of the Good Samaritan is principally a parable, and clearly no great issue is at stake in that decision. Nevertheless, it shows that the reader of the Bible does have to decide how he will understand even a narrative passage, and sometimes that decision is more difficult and carries wider implications. Is the story of Job, for instance, an account of historical events, or an extended parable not unlike the Good Samaritan? Did Jonah actually travel to Nineveh, get swallowed by a fish, and sit under the shade of a climbing gourd? Or is the whole story also a parable, about disobedience and repentance and the value of the sinner in the sight of God?

To answer those questions requires more than a simple faith in the inspiration of the Bible. After all, the story of the Good Samaritan is part of the inspired Scriptures, and conveys the truth of God, yet it does not relate (so far as we know) historical facts. Could not the parable of Job, or the parable of Jonah, coming from the pens of their inspired authors, also convey the truth of God without necessarily relating historical facts?

Questions like these are related to hermeneutics, the study of the interpretation of the Bible, and in recent years it has become clear that it is a subject which cannot be ignored by anyone who wants to take the Scriptures seriously.

The Second Vatican Council laid down new guide-lines in biblical interpretation for Roman Catholics, requiring not so much an emphasis on the historical or literal accuracy of the statements of Scripture as on the spirit and intention of the inspired writers. And the conservative evangelical world has been torn apart by heated arguments over the way in which the Bible is to be handled. The National Evangelical Anglican Congress, at Nottingham in 1977, called on its constituency to reappraise the way Scripture should be used, interpreted and preached.

All of this may seem to some Christians to be yet another unnecessary disturbance of traditional beliefs. They assume that until comparatively recently almost everybody accepted Scripture in a literal way. In fact, from as early as Origen, in the third century—and probably earlier—there have been Christian scholars who have regarded the Bible almost entirely in an allegorical sense. In the Middle Ages, hardly anybody used the Bible in a literal or historical way. The 'facts' were there solely because of the spiritual, moral or mystical truths which they represented, and every biblical statement was expected to yield (if one searched deeply enough) three levels of meaning, the moral, the allegorical and the anagogical (dealing with truths about the 'other' world).

The Protestant Reformers reacted strongly against this fanciful kind of exegesis. They insisted that the starting point in biblical interpretation should be what they called the 'literal sense' of a passage. By that they did not mean *literalism*—they were aware of the presence of allegory, parable, poetry and proverb in Scripture—but *the sense which the writer plainly intended*. The aim of their interpretation was to establish what the original writer meant to convey, judging it by the normal rules of grammar, syntax and context. They wanted to discover the plain, natural sense of each passage, and to discover what the Holy Spirit was saying to them through it. As Dr J. I. Packer has said,[1] this was essentially a 'protest against the arbitrary imposition of inapplicable literary categories on scriptural statements'.

Now few, if any, today would deny that the biblical interpretation of Origen and Chrysostom, and the medieval scholars, was fanciful in the extreme. It is highly unlikely,

[1] In *Fundamentalism and the Word of God* (IVP 1958)

for instance, that the Gospel writers really intended the 'two pennies' given by the Good Samaritan to the inn-keeper to represent the gift of the sacraments of baptism and the eucharist to the Church, as Chrysostom suggested.

On the other hand, many would claim today that there is a much stronger element of allegory and poetry in the Scriptures, even in some parts which, like the Gospels, *look* like historical accounts, than the Reformers—and more particularly some of their successors—have allowed. In reaction against fanciful allegory, and latterly against nine-teenth-century liberalism, conservative Protestants swung over to an unimaginative literalism, to which many readers of the Bible today still cling, and consequently miss (as I shall argue) that very sense 'which the original writers intended'.

One unfortunate result is that those who wish to believe in any viable theory of the inspiration of Scripture feel themselves caught in a trap. If they say that the inspired writers could only write the truth, because the Holy Spirit cannot tell a lie, and then interpret 'truth' in a literal and historical way, they are compelled frequently to maintain that something is so over against the evidence of history, science and even common sense. On the other hand, if they appear to concede that 'truth' does not necessarily involve historical or literal accuracy, then they feel that they have surrendered the argument to the liberals, because it becomes a personal decision as to which statements in the Scriptures are historical, and which are not. The first course leads to spiritual schizophrenia, the second to doctrinal confusion. One way, what God has revealed in Scripture is seen to be in conflict with what God has revealed in creation, history or reason. The other way, what God has revealed is apparently put at the mercy of whatever is the latest fad of liberal scholarship.

Just to state the dilemma is to underline how important hermeneutics is today, and how impossible it is to ignore the issues raised by it. We shall never again be in a situation in which the vast majority of people in the western world simply accepted the Bible at its face value, believing its history, its biology, its physics, its astronomy and its cosmology. For better or worse, the modern reader comes to the Bible with a more sophisticated, more critical—perhaps even more cynical—approach. He is also aware, very often, that ancient writings cannot be read as though they were modern ones, or judged by the literary, historical or scientific criteria of today.

And so, for better or worse, the modern reader needs more help in interpreting the words he reads and the ideas they convey. A vast cultural gap yawns between him and the biblical writings. A good modern translation may make their words contemporary, but it will not solve the problems raised in his mind by their ideas. The only alternative to helping him to re-think his approach to the Bible is to accept a widespread and growing disillusionment with the Bible. A minority will continue to accept it uncritically at what appears to be its literal value. A majority will not. That is not a situation to be welcomed by anyone who believes that the Bible is the means by which God speaks to all men.

That is the starting point for our approach to hermeneutics: that God has spoken. It is a fundamental principle to every orthodox Christian that Christianity is revealed rather than discovered. It is a response to a God who has spoken.

Many of the world's great religions begin with the ideas and visions of their founders—the words of Confucius or the Buddha. These ideas then become the means of a search—man's search for God. But Christianity rests upon the idea that God, who is infinite and personal, has revealed to the human race enough about himself, about itself, and about the life which people find themselves living on this planet, for them to make sense of existence, and to come to a true and satisfying relationship with their Creator. The initiative is with God—God's search for man.

This concept actually follows from belief in a God who is all-powerful and good. It is unthinkable that a God who is good (and therefore wills the best for his creatures) and all-powerful (and therefore able to carry it out) should place intelligent and sensitive beings in a strange, baffling and apparently meaningless environment, and then leave them to 'sweat it out'. Apart from a revelation from 'beyond', how on earth can any kind of meaning be given to the universe in which we live—not in the scientific sense, but in the sense of any ultimate meaning or purpose? We come from darkness and disappear, after a brief season, into darkness, and are surrounded all our days by mysteries that have baffled the greatest minds of our race.

But Christians believe (as, indeed, do Jews and Muslims) that God has not left us without a revelation from 'beyond', that he is a God who *speaks*, and that what he says is adequate, authentic and accessible. For Christians he 'speaks' through creation; he 'speaks' through Israel and her history; he 'speaks' through the prophets of Israel, and 'in these last days he has spoken to us through his Son'.[2] And still today he 'speaks' through the Church, the body of Christ on earth, revealing himself in each new situation or need.

Now all these 'words' of God are not equally reliable. The 'word' through creation, referred to by St Paul in his letter to the Romans,[3] is obscured by superstition and ignorance. The 'word' through the contemporary Church is weakened by its disunity and disagreements. The most reliable 'words'

[2] Hebrews 1:1,2
[3] Romans 1:19,20

are obviously those which are written down, because they put the revelation into a permanent form, which can be referred to and interpreted, but not altered.

Yet the written 'Word' in the Bible is more than just a reliable record of certain moments when God 'spoke'. Christians believe that it carries the authority of God himself. Its writers were 'moved by the Holy Spirit'. What they wrote are 'the words of God'.[4]

That authority all stems from one hub, the very centre of God's revelation to the human race, Jesus Christ. He is, in fact, called the 'Word' of God[5]—God's perfect self-expression in human terms. His life, death and resurrection, and his words and teaching, are unique in the *quality* of their revelation of God.

But more than that: Jesus himself gives authority to the rest of the Scriptures. He clearly regarded the Old Testament as the inspired Word of God, which 'could not be broken'[6], and which he himself had come not to contradict but to complete. And equally clearly he authorised his apostles to record for the Church of the future everything that he had taught,[7] so that Acts, the Epistles and the Revelation of St John have a kind of secondary authority of Christ—they are his words and actions reported, reflected on and lived out by the apostles he had chosen and the Church they had founded.

So it was entirely proper for the Church finally to recognise not only the four Gospels, but also the rest of the New Testament, as we now have it, as fully and authentically the Word of God in the same way as the Old Testament.

That is why for orthodox Christians Jesus Christ is the key to the inspiration of the Scriptures. Believing in a God

[4] 2 Peter 1:21
[5] John 1:14
[6] John 10:35
[7] John 14:26

who *reveals* himself, they find that revelation authenticated from beginning to end by the one they believe to be the Son of God, and himself the peak and perfection of all that God has to say to us. It is because of our faith in Christ that we cannot treat the Bible lightly, or regard it as 'just another book'. Whatever else we may decide about its interpretation, we shall see it from first to last as the Word of God, the message to our race of a God who speaks.

That message, as I said earlier, must be adequate, authentic and accessible. Its authenticity, as we have seen, depends upon the authority of Christ. If that sounds to the agnostic like a circular argument, one can only say that it is the personal encounter with the risen Christ that breaks the circle, and that that is, of course, a matter of faith. The act of believing that Jesus is the Son of God gives him, as a logical consequence, divine authority.

God's message to us must also be accessible. There would be no point in a revelation that the great majority of people would never have a hope of hearing, or of understanding if they did hear it. This is in fact a crucial point about revelation as Christians understand it, for from the very first proclamation of the Gospel, on the day of Pentecost in Jerusalem, it has been a direct appeal to the ordinary people, backed up by the direct message of the Scriptures, and evoking an immediate response.

It did not need then, and should not now, a whole hierarchy of interposed interpreters who alone fully understand it and who alone are qualified to interpret it to the people. That is not to say that the Bible is to be subject to private or individualistic interpretation, an error rejected by the New Testament writers themselves,[8] but that every Christian has access to the revelation and is entitled to check what he is told by the Church against the written record to

[8] 2 Peter 1:20

see that it is authentic. The Bereans, having heard the Christian message from no less an authority than St Paul himself, were commended for checking what he had said against the (Old Testament) Scriptures, 'to see whether these things were so'.[9]

If the Scriptures are to be accessible to people of different cultures, races and languages, and at different times in human history, then obviously they must be couched in words that speak with equal clarity to an illiterate nomad or a highly educated western city-dweller. They must be accessible to rich and poor, to the intellectual and the simple, to modern man and to medieval man. There must be nothing of substance in the Scriptures which is expressed in a form which obscures its meaning from the people of any culture or community in the world.

In effect, that means that their essential message must be capable of being understood in many ways and at different levels, without the message itself being distorted.

Obviously a sixth-century Irishman (say) would understand the Genesis creation stories differently from a twentieth-century American scientist, but the essential message—that God created all that is and within that creation gave human beings the possibility of a special relationship with himself—should come to both with equal force and authority. For the message itself to be accessible, it is necessary—not just preferable—that it should be couched in the timeless form of a story rather than the transient form of contemporary scientific language. As we shall see later, to expect the Bible to fill the role of a modern textbook of science, astronomy or history is to limit it severely. It would then only be accessible to a small section of twentieth-century people. To all the rest of the human race, past and present, it would be a closed book.

[9] Acts 17:11

So the revelation in Scripture must be authentic and accessible. It must also be adequate—that is to say, it must be sufficient to meet all the reasonable needs of a person who is seeking the truth of God. The revelation would be inadequate if it left any fundamental question unanswered— if it failed to explain who God is, what he requires of us and what he has done for us. If God has revealed himself, it is illogical to believe that he has done so in an inadequate way. It *must* be sufficient to achieve his purpose.

But to say that Scripture is authentic, adequate and accessible only tells us that God has spoken effectively. It does not say that we are hearing him correctly. That involves our interpretation of what we read, and how we should do that is the subject of the next chapter.

4: WHAT DOES IT SAY AND WHAT DOES IT MEAN?

The first and most basic question when we turn to the interpretation of a passage of Scripture is, of course, 'What does it say?' Now this may seem obvious, and simple. Of course we need to know what the words say, and of course we have excellent translations to hand which enable us to do so. And in fact the modern reader is much better placed than his predecessors in this respect. Indeed, he has little excuse for misunderstanding the literal meaning of the sentences before him.

That makes it all the more reprehensible that so many preachers and speakers (to say nothing of the authors of devotional aids to the Bible, and so on) so frequently get it wrong, sometimes through carelessness, but often, one feels, because they are using the Scriptures to advance an argument or urge a response, rather than concentrating on establishing what the words actually say.

I recall one speaker justifying the practice of consuming the remains of the communion wine at the end of the service by quoting our Lord's words, 'Drink ye *all of this*', whereas grammar and context require the meaning, 'Drink this, *all of you*.'

I wonder how many sermons have been based on the words in Job: 'I know that my redeemer liveth . . . and though worms destroy my body, yet in my flesh shall I see God.'

Yet that last clause is almost exactly the opposite of what the text actually means: 'Yet *without* my flesh I shall see God'—as any modern translation will confirm.

Those are, of course, simply examples either of mistranslation (and there are about seven hundred similar examples in the Authorised Version) or of a misunderstanding of an ambiguous translation. Very often, in order to establish exactly what the original writer said, we shall need to look at more than one translation, and even, in the case of a really difficult verse, a Bible commentary. Even that will not solve some of the problems. There are still a few verses in the Old Testament where nobody knows for sure what the original writer intended, though the number is steadily decreasing.

One of them gave me a wry moment of pleasure a few years ago. A militantly Protestant preacher in a mission hall was weighing in against ritualism and 'priestcraft'. He was particularly scornful of those who wear what he called 'fancy robes': 'We need none of those things here,' he claimed. 'We look to the Scriptures, and "worship the Lord in the beauty of holiness".' Unhappily for him, he had hit on one of the most felicitous mistranslations in the Authorised Bible.

The psalmist was actually exhorting—as in the previous example—almost exactly the opposite of what the preacher was commending: 'Worship the Lord in holy array'—in other words, put on the 'fancy robes' of the Temple and carry out the priestly rites of worship.

A more culpable misuse of the Bible, which also serves to

distort what it actually says, is the modern equivalent of the old allegorical approach. I remember a preacher at the Keswick Convention 'for the deepening of the spiritual life' taking the story of Jesus healing the woman who had been 'bent double' for many years.[1] In the course of his address we were told that one of her sins was that she had been 'introspective'—'turned in on herself'. This original interpretation was based on the statement that she was 'bent in upon herself'—that is, in plain English, that her back was curved. The literal sense is made quite clear in the verse in question: 'She could not fully straighten herself.' To take a factual description of a physical affliction and use it to clinch an argument that has no connection at all with the passage in question is, to my mind, a scandalous misuse of the Scriptures.

One more example of this kind of misuse must suffice for now. I take it from one of the best-known religious books of the sixties, *Honest to God*, where John Robinson uses a phrase from the parable of the prodigal son to clinch an argument which is central to the whole book, that man can encounter God when he turns back within himself to the 'ground of his being', where 'God' exists in that which is most precious and important to him. So Robinson sees the 'new creation' as occurring when, like the prodigal son, we 'come to ourselves'—discover, in effect, the 'ground of our being'.

But in fact the turning point of the story—as any reader can verify[2]—is not then, but when, having determined to 'arise and go to his father', he *actually does so*. He might well have 'come to himself'—which only means, in context, that he saw the truth of his position—and done nothing about it. It is his repentance ('I have sinned against heaven and before

[1] Luke 13:10–13
[2] Luke 15:11–24

you') and return to the father that is the actual turning point. Once again, it seems to me, some other over-riding aim has led the author to *use* the Scripture rather than deal with it on the basis of what it actually says. All exposition of the Bible must start at the right place—establishing what the words say—even if the expositor is, like Dr Robinson, one of the foremost New Testament scholars of his day. Only then can the other criteria be applied to establish the various levels of meaning.

The first of these 'other criteria' is the historical and social context of the passage. Just as we cannot understand the character of Shylock, in *The Merchant of Venice*, without knowing something of the place of Jews, and the common attitude towards them in medieval Europe, so we cannot expect to understand the Old Testament prophets, or the Psalms, or even the Gospels, without some knowledge of their historical and religious background.

An extreme example of the problems created by ignoring this is the way many fundamentalists, especially in America, approach the Book of Revelation. Apocalyptic literature, as it is called, was a familiar literary form in New Testament times. It was never intended to be a timetable guide to the future, yet this is how the literalists insist on reading it. 'Revelation' is, like all apocalyptic literature, a series of evocative pictures, largely based on contemporary events, on the theme of the judgment and eventual triumph of God. It contains a good many allusions to contemporary powers and tyrants, often hidden in elaborate verbal or numerical codes, but uses them as 'building materials' in the creation of a total picture, a picture which can only be understood when viewed *as a whole*.

So to speculate on the present-day or future identity of the Scarlet Woman, or the four horsemen, or the various kingdoms who war with each other in the battle of Armageddon, is simply a nonsense. No such future identification was intended by the writer, and no such identification is possible now.

Equally, to argue—and even excommunicate fellow-Christians—over the details of the millennium, and whether it is to follow or precede such and such another event, is also a nonsense. It is like arguing that Britain's greatness is to be gained with bows of burning gold and arrows of desire (and even disputing about their size and shape), on the basis of statements in Blake's prophetic poem, 'Jerusalem'.

For his contemporaries, the seer of the Revelation was speaking familiar language, using a familiar literary form. They would not have been so perverse as to think that he was mapping out the future of Europe in detail. They would have known that he was using topical events and people to illustrate eternal truths, and also using the most powerful symbols he could draw on (a woman in labour, armed horsemen, plague and pestilence) to convey the drama of the cosmic struggle between God and the adversary, between good and evil, and the ultimate divine victory and destruction of 'the devil and his angels'.

Incidentally, this also means that the ordinary reader can 'understand' Revelation as well as the scholar. It needs no complicated time charts or detailed knowledge of ancient history. All it really needs is some imagination.

The Gospels probably represent the most controversial part of the Bible where the question of historical and social context is concerned. To the modern reader, there appears at first sight to be no problem. We seem to be moving in a familiar world, peopled with the kind of characters we have all met—anxious fathers, bereaved mothers, over-confident young men, religious hypocrites. The literary form also seems familiar, not unlike the more colourful kind of history book.

But into this 'familiar' world, and into what reads like a straight-forward historical account, walks the amazing figure of Jesus.

Suddenly the everyday feel is in sharp tension with supernatural events. Water is turned into wine, thousands are fed with five bread rolls and two sardines, dead bodies are raised, water is walked upon. And finally, of course, as though to cap it all, a coolly historical account of a political trial and execution is followed by an equally cool account of the victim coming back from the dead to outwit his adversaries.

So the modern reader finds himself in a strangely contra-dictory position. The setting and style of the Gospels *seem* familiar to us, but the supernatural element catches us by surprise. We are left at times with the feeling that there are two accounts here: one of people and events of a natural and familiar order, and another of a world with which we are totally unfamiliar.

Now undoubtedly part of this difficulty is created by the person of Jesus. If he was, as Christians believe, the incarnate Son of God, human and divine, then we should expect that his presence on earth would be marked by extraordinary events. Given the foundational miracle of the incarnation, there is nothing intrinsically incredible, nor even particularly surprising, about the Gospel miracles.

But biblical scholars are increasingly unwilling to leave it at that, and in one respect, at least, they can help us to understand the Gospels better. Their major debate is over the apparently innocuous question, 'What *is* a Gospel?' and there is no doubt that to find an answer to that question will go a long way to solving many of the perplexities of the modern reader who approaches these books.

In the nineteenth and early twentieth century it was fairly generally assumed that the Gospels were written in the literary form of first-century biographies—a common *genre* in the Graeco-Roman world. But in the twenties, and increasingly under the influence of Bultmann, there was a swing away from this view, so that for forty years or more the prevailing view has been that the Gospels are *not* biographies of Jesus, but narrative versions of the apostolic *kerygma*—that is to say, the message which the early church proclaimed. This view of the Gospels starts in fact with the 'Gospel', the message preached by St Peter, St Paul and their successors, and it assumes, correctly of course, that this message preceded the writing of the Gospels. Then the Gospels are seen as the clothing of this 'core' of the Gospel with vivid narrative, each incident illustrating in a memorable way some aspect of the truth about Jesus which the early Church had experienced. As literary works, they were unique in the ancient world—*sui generis*.

This idea of the Gospels as providing a 'mythical structure' which could convey the full force of the impact of Jesus on his contemporaries and their successors sounds more complicated than it is, but there is no doubt that it evacuates the Gospels of anything remotely like historical reliability. Almost any event or saying recorded in them can be interpreted as a kind of visual aid to the understanding of Jesus, *and no more*. And that applies not only to miracles like the feeding of the five thousand, or the miraculous draught of fishes, but even to the resurrection itself.

More recently, however, there has been yet another swing of scholarly opinion, away from the view that the Gospels are not biographies, towards the view that this, in fact, is exactly what they are[3]—sharing the style and structure of many Graeco-Roman biographies. That is not to say that they are identical with modern biographies, but it is to say

[3] See, for instance, *What is a Gospel?* by Charles H. Talbert (SPCK 1978)

that they set out to present an accurate and informative portrait of their subject, Jesus of Nazareth, and the significance of his teaching and actions. Far from being unique in their literary form, they follow a recognisable form and so could have been understood and accepted by their first readers.

This idea of the Gospels as biographies—even if in antiquity's genre—can be a considerable help to the modern reader coming to them. Once we see the Gospels as primarily portraits of Jesus, using various literary devices and forms to add colour, depth and meaning to the picture, we shall have a far more dynamic approach to them. We shall expect to find different emphases between the four—as we should in four biographies of, say, Winston Churchill—and also fundamental differences of approach. But because they are the products of their age, we shall also not be surprised to find, even in a biography, elements of poetry, allegory and midrash.

'Midrash' is the unfamiliar word in that list to most modern readers, yet it is a commonplace in the discussions of the academics. Because it is a literary device of one period of history, and because it is not employed today, most of us are unaware of its existence, or if we are, how deeply it affects our interpretation of much of the Bible.

A midrash is a story woven around a prophecy, or some other profound spiritual statement. The rabbis of our Lord's time used it to put flesh and bones on abstract ideas, to turn concepts into vivid, colourful narrative. They would certainly have reacted indignantly to any suggestion that they were being dishonest, or telling lies. As they saw it, they were illustrating and applying truth through stories—serving the truth, bringing it home, making it more immediate. Their readers (or hearers), of course, knew what they were doing, and would never have been so perverse as to accuse them of distorting history, or spreading misleading information about historical figures. We shall be looking at some examples of midrash later on.

The important thing about establishing the various literary devices that the biblical writers employed and the cultural influences on them, is not just to indulge in an academic exercise, but to establish *what the writers intended to convey to their readers*. All through, that is the primary principle. It may well be that some scholars have had a field day discovering this and that allusion or uncovering hints of this or that influence on the biblical text. Undoubtedly, too, after the manner of scholars in all disciplines, they have often 'discovered' things that are not really there, and seen connections where no connections exist. But the fact that we can set one scholar against another, and show without much difficulty that they often contradict each other, does not mean that we should shut our eyes to their work.

Good biblical scholarship is vital to enable modern readers to understand the Bible correctly, and it is sheer obscurantism to pretend that 'anyone can pick up the Bible and understand it perfectly'. Of course there is a core of the 'message' of the Bible that is clear and plain to any reader, and with a certain amount of help, a smattering of humility and an average amount of imagination, ninety per cent or more of the Bible is within the comprehension of any literate human being. But that 'certain amount of help' is vital, as the Ethiopian eunuch in the book of the Acts realised,[4] and those who refuse it may well miss—or misunderstand—a great deal of what the Bible has to say to them.

So, when we turn to the text of the Bible itself, certain questions have to be faced if we are to do it justice. The first is, what does it actually say? To answer that adequately, we shall have to ask what literary form it is in (is it allegory,

[4] Acts 8:31

43

poetry, apocalyptic, history?), and what its context is. The context is not simply the few sentences either side of it, but the historical, social and cultural setting (when was it written, for whom, and with what intention?). When we have established, to the best of our ability, what the passage actually says, we shall be able to answer the most important question of all—what is it intended to say to *me, now*? That involves us in an exercise of faith, because we believe that this piece of writing is inspired by the Holy Spirit. But it also involves an exercise in imagination, as we allow the 'message', couched perhaps in unfamiliar terms and literary forms, to penetrate our twentieth-century pre-suppositions and speak to us in a dynamic and personal way.

5: IN THE BEGINNING, WHAT?

In this chapter and the next I should like to try to apply the principles discussed so far to two biblical stories which are typical of those which cause modern readers difficulty, the creation story, and then the Gospel accounts of the birth of Jesus.

The creation story in Genesis, and the stories of Noah and the Flood and the tower of Babel which follow it, have been arenas of conflict for over a century. The number of those who still take them literally, or as history, is small, but vociferous. Indeed, in recent years the vocal and well-organised evolution protest movement has managed to persuade quite a large number of young evangelicals that belief in the historicity of the creation account in Genesis is an essential part of orthodox Christianity. And the influential Dr Francis Schaeffer, as we have already seen, has made belief in the historical reliability of the first eleven chapters of Genesis an esssential foundation for the whole Christian revelation.

This has always seemed to me a peculiarly perverse and unhelpful approach, which owes more to modern conditioning than respect for the Scriptures. We do not know who the author or authors of this part of the Bible were, but the one thing that seems certain is that they did not set out to write an historical account of verifiable events (like a modern newspaper reporting an earthquake or a revolution), but to record, under the inspiration of the Holy Spirit, the truth about the origins of the universe, of life, of man, and of evil.

It is only the prosaic mind of modern man that cannot see how truth ('true truth', in Schaeffer's tautology) can be better expressed in pictures, symbols and story than in science, statistics and analysis.

I would suggest a simple experiment. Pick up a Bible and read the first three chapters of Genesis *as though you had come across them for the first time*. Try to eradicate preconceived ideas about them, and forget all you have been told or read on the subject. Then ask yourself how it comes across, even to a literally-minded modern reader. Does it sound like a science textbook, or a paper on the origins of life, or a dissertation on cosmology? Do Adam and Eve (or 'the man' and 'the woman' as modern translations correctly call them) sound like actual historical characters, like King David or Julius Caesar?

More importantly, are those actually the questions that come to your mind? I very much doubt it. It would be a very dull and unimaginative person who could read the magnificent opening sentences of the Bible and ask, But surely the 'heaven' existed *before* the 'earth'? or, What precisely is the 'deep'? or, Where did the 'light' come from before the sun was created?

I can never read those solemn sentences, among the most profound and mind-stretching ever written, without a feeling of awe: 'In the beginning, God created the heaven and the earth. And the earth was without form and void, and darkness was upon the face of the deep; and the Spirit of

God was moving over the face of the waters. And God said, "Let there be light"; and there was light . . .' I would find the power and authority of those words infinitely diminished if I believed that they were simply a statement of observable fact. Truth at this kind of level is too subtle, too profound, too *important* to be captured in the banal language of the historical reporter.

However, the modern reader conducting this experiment will also have noticed a few other things. In the first place, it is obvious that there is a poetic form or pattern to the account of creation, with a recurring refrain: 'Evening came, and morning came, the first day.' God speaks, and his word has creative power. Six times he speaks, and on the seventh 'day' he rests, and everything that his word has called into being is 'very good'.

Then he will have noticed that the author, who was obviously not unintelligent, is not bothered by the fact that he is measuring time in 'days' before the creation of the sun. He was, of course, perfectly well aware that sunrise and sunset are the boundaries of the day, but that did not prevent him from using the word 'day'—though clearly he did not intend it to be understood as representing twenty-four hours. In fact, the word he used could be translated 'time' or even 'age'. Only a modern literalist would try to argue that Genesis envisaged a world created in six periods of twenty-four hours.

But alongside these factual discrepancies, the reader who comes to Genesis with imagination and faith will find a story of such power and seriousness that to argue about them would seem like blasphemy. The writer of Genesis was not concerned with asking *how* creation occurred but with bearing witness to the fact that it did, and that its first cause, designer and executor was God. Every detail of the story, every brush-stroke in the picture, serves that purpose. It is

47

the reader's responsibility to bring imagination and faith to his reading, going along with the writer's purpose, not superimposing on it an alien intention.

It is a distortion, and a diminution, of these creation stories to ignore the poetry, shut one's eyes to the drama and concentrate on the very things that the writer could not possibly have regarded as important: the order of events and the scientific method of creation.

Take, for instance, the stories of the creation of man and woman. The man, we are told, is formed 'of the dust of the ground'. It would be hard to think of a single phrase that could convey so much so vividly about the nature of man's physical existence. The very word 'dust' has become part of the poetry of human existence. 'For dust thou art, and unto dust shalt thou return' . . . 'he remembers that we are but dust' . . . 'ashes to ashes, dust to dust . . .'

Some writers and preachers have attempted to prove that the statement about man being created 'from the dust of the ground' is literally true, and have produced various lists of chemicals which constitute the human body, to 'prove' the truth of the Bible. Now it may, or may not, be a fact that there is a chemical truth here. But that is trivial compared to the infinitely greater truth that the phrase enshrines: that man is part of his environment, 'of the earth, earthy'—not an angel, but a part of the created planet, as real as the dust of the ground but also, apart from his spirit, as insignificant. There is a whole theology of the body in that one metaphor.

The woman, according to Genesis, was formed of a rib taken from the man's body by God while he slept. There may still be a few readers of the Bible who are worried by the fact that this was *not* how the female half of the species originated—that is to say, it was not the method, the 'how'. As a matter of literal, observable, scientific fact, we know about as certainly as we can know anything that woman was

48

not formed of a part of the male body—the truth lies, if anything, in the precise opposite.

Yet at a deeper level altogether, this story tells us more about the interrelation of the sexes than any merely scientific 'explanation' could hope to do. Vividly, memorably, it shows the common life of the sexes, their interdependence, their lack of completeness without the other.

It also, in its most moving description of the role of the woman in relation to the man—as a companion and supporter—gives the basis of the biblical theology of the sexes. Science can tell us a lot about the way in which male and female roles in reproduction come about, but Genesis puts the whole thing in a far more splendid, profound and significant light. This is a truth *greater than* factual accuracy.

The same is true of probably the most profound allegory in the whole of human literature, the Garden of Eden and the Fall. Enormous volumes have been written on the problem of the origin of evil. Few are satisfying; many are almost completely incomprehensible to the average person. But the writer of Genesis, inspired by the Holy Spirit, puts it all into a story—a story which a child can follow, but so profound that it can satisfy the most brilliant mind.

From the economy of language—the story employs a vocabulary of disarming simplicity—to the magnificence of the setting ('the Lord God planted a garden eastward in Eden . . .') we are moving in the realms of ultimate truth. Every image is archetypal: the Tree of Life, the cunning serpent, the gullible woman, the weak man, the guilt and secrecy, the inevitable uncovering of disobedience and the expulsion from the idyllic garden. It is a story that, no matter how many times I read it, still moves me profoundly.

I could never despise it, nor treat it frivolously. For me, there is nothing funny about the serpent, or the forbidden fruit or the fig leaves, but only the stark tragedy of the abuse of freedom and the rejection of the highest for the sake of the illusion of power.

Read like that, it seems again to verge on blasphemy to start an argument about whether 'Adam' and 'Eve' were actual historical characters. 'Adam' simply means 'the man', and 'Eve' means 'Life'. Throughout the story of the Garden of Eden and the Fall, they are described simply as 'the man' and 'the woman', as any modern translation will testify. Not until after the judgment of their disobedience and their expulsion from Eden are they given the proper names 'Adam' and 'Eve'. This seems to me to put into perspective an argument which worries some Christians: that St Paul's comparison of Adam and Christ puts them on a similar level of historicity. 'As in Adam all die, so in Christ all will be brought to life . . . The first man, Adam, became an animate being, whereas the last Adam has become a life-giving spirit.'[1]

Here again the confusion seems to be over the purpose of the writer. Paul was not speaking here of scientific or historical facts, but of ultimate, theological truth. After all, the name of the Christ was 'Jesus', not 'Adam', but nobody worries over that rather daring use of metaphor. The first man—whoever and whenever he was—had the body of an animal; the 'last man' (not literally, you notice, but theologically) is a life-giving spirit. 'Observe,' says the apostle, 'the spiritual does not come first; the animal body comes first, and then the spiritual . . . The man made of dust is the pattern of all men made of dust, and the heavenly man is the pattern of all the heavenly.'[2] Could anyone seriously argue that that profound unveiling of the ultimate truth about man's meaning and destiny is dependent upon a literal and historical Adam and Eve? It is, surely, at a different

[1] I Corinthians 15:22,45
[2] I Corinthians 15:46,48

level of truth altogether, and it seems to me to trivialise it to use it in an argument about biological origins.

Probably there was, in some distant primeval setting, a first human couple, gifted, unlike their predecessors, with a human spirit capable of responding to their Creator. But the question is, literally, irrelevant. The Fall is observable fact—we *are* fallen. The story of the Garden of Eden explains not how man fell (that is to say, the mechanics) but *why* man fell. It answers, in the only way our minds can comprehend, the most important questions raised by that fact—who is responsible: God, the devil, or ourselves? And it provides the only credible explanation for a truth about existence which is plain to everyone who looks honestly at the world around us—that the world is beautiful, but spoilt by evil, and that man is significant, but lost. For the explanation of that mystery I, for one, find more help in the story of the Garden of Eden than in all the writings of the philosophers and theologians.

So we can move on. The story of Noah and the Flood almost certainly has an element of historical truth about it, but the tell-tale addition of the promise attached to the rainbow should warn us against a literalistic approach. After the Flood, according to Genesis, God said, 'I set my bow in the cloud, and it shall be a sign of the covenant between me and the earth . . . and the waters shall never again become a flood to destroy all flesh.' Obviously there had been rainbows before the Flood, but God used an existing phenomenon—as he did bread and wine in the eucharist— to signify a new relationship. That is the *truth* of the story of the rainbow, a truth about the covenant between the Creator and his creatures. That truth is not affected by the historicity or otherwise of the Flood itself, or the other details of the story.

Finally, in these opening chapters of Genesis, we can turn

51

to the story of the tower of Babel. The men who decided to build this tower had 'few words' and 'one language'. As a result, unsurprisingly, they were able to work well together. The Lord 'came down' to see the city and the tower that they were building, and decided that a united human race was a threat to his sovereignty: 'This is only the beginning of what they will do; and nothing that they propose to do will now be impossible for them.'

So God 'confused their language' and 'scattered them abroad from there over the face of all the earth', and the tower, the symbol of human pride and achievement, was presumably left to dilapidate.

There is probably no story in the Bible that so clearly illustrates the difference between 'myth'—rightly understood—and 'history'. Quite obviously this story is not history. We know for certain that the development of different languages is a slow, gradual process—one that is, of course, still going on. The divergence of language is the result of human migration, not the cause of it. That is to say, when people separate and move away, eventually, over a long period of time, their language changes.

As usual, however, there are elements of history in the story, and also, more importantly, deeper and wider truths. It is very likely that civilisation had its roots in this fertile corner of the earth, and the building of ziggurats and other towers was common in the pre-Abramic period. It is true also, at that deeper level, that language has been a powerful factor in human disunity, leading to endless misunderstandings, prejudices and hatred; and that as human beings spread over the continents, so their languages became more and more tribal and national badges, separating them ever more effectively from the rest of their race.

What the story of Babel does is to take an observable phenomenon—that the human race is divided by language—

and provide an explanation which combines such historical elements as the story-teller can glean and the deeper insights into human behaviour and motivation which the inspiration of the Holy Spirit adds. The result is a story which telescopes into one powerful incident, memorably related, a process which in fact took tens of thousands of years, and uses it to convey an important truth about man and his condition.

All of that is fairly obvious in this story. The building of towers, for instance, did not occur at the time when mankind was beginning to develop language. But it helps us also to understand a principle of these ancient writings which our twentieth-century conditioning often finds difficult. Just as the Tower of Babel story telescopes thousands of years of linguistic history in order to make a profoundly true point about man, so the Creation story telescopes millions of years of scientific history to make a profoundly true point about God. In neither case is it true to call the story 'fiction'; and in neither case can it be called 'history'. It is, most simply, truth clothed in a timeless form, and made accessible to all those who have imagination and faith.

6: WHAT HAPPENED AT BETHLEHEM?

The great majority of Christians, including many who hold a high view of biblical inspiration, find no great difficulty in accepting that the opening chapters of Genesis are not recording literal history. After all, and despite the strident protests of the anti-evolution lobby, most educated people have some idea of the evidence about the age of the earth, about its fossil record, and about the broad outline of the evolution of life on this planet. The fact that scientists argue over details, and even nowadays question the hitherto sacrosanct doctrines of Charles Darwin, does not constitute any sort of a case for throwing reason to the winds and denying the evidence of nearly two hundred years of meticulous and painstaking research. So Christians, faced with a literature that to a reasonable mind looks like allegory, and with a science that virtually rules out treating it as history, have for the most part accepted the sort of conclusions I outlined in the last chapter.

Some, of course, have gone further, and give Genesis little more authority than the pagan creation myths of the Near East. Others, fearful for the doctrine of biblical inerrancy,

54

have refused to concede that these chapters are anything other than divinely dictated history. For me, the first position is only tenable if any effective doctrine of inspiration has been jettisoned, and I see no grounds whatever for doing that. The second seems to me to be the spiritual equivalent of King Canute, desperately and bravely trying to hold off the inevitable. It also, as I have already argued at length, does less than justice to the intention of the inspired writers, and represents a narrow, unimaginative and essentially mechanical approach to the Word of God.

But the New Testament nativity narratives represent a different kind of problem. Here we have the biblical accounts, by Matthew and Luke, of the birth of Jesus. Central doctrines of Christianity are built upon the event of the incarnation, the coming of Christ into the world and into human flesh. Indeed, one could say that the most fundamental doctrine of the faith, that Jesus Christ is the incarnate Son of God, has its roots in the story of his birth of the virgin Mary at Bethlehem. It is not surprising that many Christians, not all of them fundamentalists by any means, jib at questioning, or even discussing, the historical basis of these accounts.

Not only that, but we have invested a great deal of emotional capital in the Christmas story. More than any other Christian festival, certainly in the West, it has become identified with family and home, with peace and goodwill, with generosity and human love. In many Western countries the biggest congregations of the year turn out for carol services and midnight masses, and the crib, the archetypal symbol of the loving, united family, is in shop windows as well as church alcoves.

So naturally people feel threatened when scholars hint (or do more than hint) that part at least of these familiar narratives is not historically true. They do not want to hear, as various writers have alleged, that Jesus was not born of a virgin, was not visited by Wise Men, was not carried away into Egypt, was not born under a travelling star and was not born in Bethlehem at all, but Nazareth.

Let me hasten to say that that is not a consensus of responsible scholarly opinion, as we shall shortly see. But it does indicate a willingness on the part of many theologians, and in some cases a quite cruel eagerness, to shatter some of the most deeply held and emotionally engaging beliefs about the incarnation of Jesus. In the face of it, the inevitable double reaction occurs. Some Christians have gone. all the way with the most extreme sceptics, and more or less evacuated the biblical stories of any historical ground at all—beyond, of course, the obvious fact that Jesus must have been born somewhere, at some date on the calendar. Others have swung to the opposite extreme, employing enormous ingenuity to try to harmonise the obvious discrepancies between the two accounts and arguing that every detail is literally and historically true.

The fact is that the discrepancies between Matthew's account of the birth of Jesus, and Luke's, are enormous. Indeed, a reader coming freshly to both accounts might be forgiven for assuming that they are describing different events. Matthew, like Luke, asserts that Jesus was born of a virgin mother, Mary, in Bethlehem, but they appear to differ over all the rest of the details. Luke says that Mary and Joseph lived in Nazareth and travelled to Bethlehem for a census decreed by the Emperor Augustus. Matthew appears to be unaware of this. For him, Joseph and Mary did not decide to live in Nazareth until long after the birth, as a result of Archelaus coming to the throne in Judaea with a consequent danger to the life of the infant Jesus.

Matthew (perhaps unimportantly) does not record the visit of the shepherds. On the other hand, Luke does not record the visit of the Wise Men. Indeed, the account by Matthew of their visit has its own internal problems. It seems incredible, for instance, that Herod's security forces should be so incompetent as to be unable to find a new-born rival in a small town a mere six miles down the road from his palace—a rival who had been visited by exotic Eastern sages. The earlier subterfuge with the Wise Men would appear to have been totally unnecessary: the prophecy of the birth of the Messiah was common knowledge, not confined to learned theologians.[1]

Luke's account of the birth of Jesus ends in a matter-of-fact way with the baby being presented in the Temple in Jerusalem, according to the law of Moses, and the family then returning to their home at Nazareth in Galilee. Matthew, on the other hand, has a rather more sensational scenario, and one apparently unknown to Luke. After an angelic warning to Joseph in a dream, the parents made a hurried night flight to Egypt with the child. There then followed Herod's slaughter of all the children in the Bethlehem area who were two years old and under, and, after the king's death, Joseph and Mary's decision to reside in Nazareth, in Galilee, as offering a safer home than Bethlehem, ruled over by Herod's son.

Now, what are we to make of all this? The first thing to say is that although the two accounts are irreconcilable in terms of facts, it does not follow that both are wrong. That would be an illogical assumption.

The second is that we should pursue exactly the same approach as we would to any other passages of Scripture. We should ask the same questions: Who is writing this? What is his intention? What literary form is it in? What is its historical, social and theological context? If we do, we may well find that the difficulties tend to solve themselves, and

[1] See and compare Matthew 2:4–6 and John 7:42.

that the list of historical discrepancies given above is almost entirely irrelevant to our understanding both of what actually happened (that is, the history) and what it means (that is, the theology).

If we apply these principles of interpretation to the two nativity stories, we shall certainly come to the conclusion that they are very different pieces of writing. It is true that both are part of a Gospel, which we have already described as a kind of biography. But in the ancient world biography took many different forms, and Matthew and Luke, although both presenting a portrait of the same person, Jesus, have a markedly different approach to the task.

Matthew's is a Gospel through Jewish eyes. Its aim is to prove that Jesus is the promised Messiah, the son of David and the Son of God. Its form is not that of chronological narrative—far from it. It is structured to present an argument (that in Jesus Judaism is fulfilled), not to report events. Everything in the Gospel serves this purpose, including the arrangement of the material. From the opening geneology, which is carefully and deliberately divided into three parts, with fourteen generations in each—the exact numerical value of the consonants in the Hebrew word 'David'—to the grouping of the sayings and actions of Jesus into five 'books of the Christ', like the five books of the Law, the reader is aware that the purpose of the writer is dictating the form and shape and content of his Gospel. Each of the five books ends with the same formula: 'When Jesus finished these sayings . . .' Parables are presented in a group of seven, the perfect number. Nine miracles are recorded in groups of three. And all through the book, as even the casual reader will see, the recurrent theme occurs: 'This was to fulfil what the prophet spoke.'

All of this serves to underline that this book is not to be read simply as an historical account of the life of Jesus of

Nazareth. Such a book probably existed long before Matthew's Gospel was written. His aim is evidenced by his structure, his selection of sayings and events, and the literary form in which he expresses himself. The book has a distinctly rabbinical flavour—it is couched in the style of the teachings and sayings of the rabbis of New Testament days—and we shall only read Matthew correctly when we read him (as far as we can) through Jewish eyes.

For example, Mark tells us that Jesus rode into Jerusalem on a donkey. Matthew knew his Old Testament, and improved on that. Zechariah had said that the Messiah would come riding on 'an ass, and on a donkey the foal of an ass', and so, in Matthew's account, that is exactly what he did.

A modern reader might feel that this is simply deception. To us, either Jesus rode on one animal or two, and it is quite important to the truth of the event to know which. To the first-century Jew, familiar with the way the rabbis used the Old Testament, there was no such feeling. As R. V. G. Tasker has written, 'To the pious Jew, the utterances of the Prophets had very much the same place in their idea of the world, as what we call the Laws of Nature have for us . . . The power of the argument from prophecy . . . was that it attempted to legitimatise the gospel history, to show that it was the legitimate outcome of the religion of holy men of old.' [2]

Matthew is full of such 'arguments from prophecy', and there is little doubt that he was following the rabbinical precedent and starting from the prophecy rather than the event. Obviously this shapes and colours his interpretation of the event itself, because he is almost obsessively concerned with the *argument*, with establishing the principle, with the

[2] *The Nature and Purpose of the Gospels* (SCM 1944)

inner truth of the life and teaching of Jesus, the son of David.

Luke, on the other hand, is equally obviously concerned first with the event, and only secondarily with its inner meaning. His purpose is set out clearly in the prologue to his Gospel. Many, he says, have set out to compile a narrative of the things which were accomplished in the ministry of Jesus, 'just as they were delivered to us by those who from the beginning were eyewitnesses and ministers of the word'. Now Luke (and in this case, at least, we may be pretty sure it *is* the work of Paul's medical friend) feels that he, 'who has followed all these things closely for some time', should himself write an '*orderly* account' of these events.

Now that is very near the modern idea of a biography, and the reader of Luke will find the territory less unfamiliar, and less opaque, than Matthew's. Although many of the same events are recorded in both—probably from the same sources, and often in the same words—the purpose of the author is quite clearly different. Luke is trying to write an accurate, reliable, chronological record. Matthew is arguing a case. There really is a world of difference between their approaches to basically the same material.

This distinction is important because, as we have seen, one of the most fundamental questions in biblical interpretation is, 'What did the original writer intend?' If it is true that the intentions of Matthew and Luke were fundamentally different, then that affects our understanding of what they wrote in a fundamental way. If Luke set out to write history, then we are entitled to read him as history, and judge him by the criteria of historical accuracy. If Matthew, on the other hand, set out to write a theological treatise, then we must judge what he wrote as theology, and apply the criteria of theological truth, as it was understood at the time when he wrote it.

Judged by those standards, both writers emerge as reliable and authoritative. Luke is clearly a careful historian, who likes to root what he reports in verifiable events (see the opening of chapter two of his Gospel). The 'feel' of the book is of restraint and modesty, and there is little doubt that he rejected a great deal of apocryphal material about the life and sayings of Jesus that was around in his day.

In preparing our radio programme on the birth narratives, we found that historians and biblical scholars were inclined to regard Luke's account as basically historical, largely because of these factors in his approach. Even over such disputed details as the governorship of Quirinius,[3] where there is some confusion over the accuracy of Luke's statement, many are prepared to give him the benefit of the doubt. At any rate, there is no doubt about his intention, and few scholars would dispute that the reader looking for an historical account of the life of Jesus, as preached and believed in the apostolic church, should take Luke, and also Mark, as his guide.

Matthew, however, is in a different category. The presence of 'midrash', as defined earlier, presents an interpretative hazard unfamiliar to the modern reader. For myself, having tried hard to find a satisfactory alternative explanation, I now have little doubt that the story of the Wise Men is a 'midrash', a beautifully imaginative story woven around various Old Testament prophecies and intended to establish that the Messiah is a King for all peoples, everywhere. Even the gentile world brings its gifts and lays them at his feet; even the highest academics of the East, the astrologers, bow before him. Every detail of the story, including the flight into Egypt and the slaughter of the innocents, is based upon prophecy, sometimes interpreted with daring originality and little regard for its historical context.

[3] Luke 2:2

61

All of this is unfamiliar ground for us, and the temptation is to apply totally irrelevant criteria of judgment to it. Matthew and his original readers would be astonished beyond words to be accused of 'inaccuracy' or 'distortion'. They were familiar with the way the rabbis would take an Old Testament prophecy and weave a story around it to draw out its inner meaning and its contemporary relevance; and they would have found these stories inspiring and perceptive in their insight into the deeper meaning of the coming into the world of the Christ.

That is how we should see them, as sermon illustrations, as pictures—visual aids, if you like—intended to illuminate the most profound mystery of all, the incarnation. Seen in that way, to tell the 'truth' is not the same thing as to relate 'facts', possibly because the recital of facts could never, at any rate for a first-century Jew, tell us all of the truth.

The most telling objection to this view of the story of the Wise Men, at any rate from the point of view of someone who believes in the inspiration of Scripture, is that it 'opens the door' to a similar treatment of more central parts of the birth narrative. Might not the Virgin Birth, for instance, be a midrash, or the location of the nativity at Bethlehem, or the connection with the line of David? After all, these too are prophesied in the Old Testament.

However, while it may be true that in the New Testament these illustrative stories are usually based upon Old Testament prophecies, it is certainly not true to argue from that that every New Testament 'event' which was prophesied in the Old Testament did not actually 'happen'. One example will prove this.

It is clearly prophesied that the Christ would be preceded by a herald or messenger.[4] But that John the Baptist 'went before' Jesus and pointed forward to him is one of the most

[4] Malachi 3:1

historically reliable facts in the New Testament. In other words, we cannot make such sweeping generalisations about the interpretation of these books. Each story, each passage, must be interpreted by the criteria we have discussed. There is simply no short cut.

If we do that, we shall find that there are a few cases where the evidence is overwhelming that we are dealing with midrash—a poetic elaboration of an Old Testament prophecy. The Wise Men and the flight into Egypt seem to be examples of this.

There will also be a few passages where the interpretation is doubtful. That is to say, there may be a midrashic 'feel', but historical or literary evidence suggests there may also be a solid historical basis for the story. The 'signs' in John's Gospel, the tearing of the Temple curtain on Good Friday, and the feeding of the five thousand might be seen as falling in this category.

For myself, in such cases the logical thing to do is to accept the historicity of the stories until proved otherwise. The story of the Wise Men sounds like midrash; but more than that, it has—as we have seen—historical inconsistencies. It does not read like history, even ancient history. But the Gospel miracles *do* read like history—they occur in identifiable places, with verifiable facts and characters.

It is not enough to argue that because they recount supernatural events they cannot be historically true. On that basis, Jesus could not be the Son of God, and his remains are somewhere in Palestine.

The Virgin Birth itself is also put in this 'doubtful' category by many otherwise conservative scholars. They see it as a story enshrining a truth revealed to the Church through the resurrection—that Jesus is the Son of God, a unique Person in his nature, human and divine. It is seen as but a step from that dawning realisation to the weaving of a miraculous birth story around a prophecy of Isaiah about a deliverer being born to a virgin. So, it is argued, we have the Gospel accounts of the birth of Jesus to the virgin Mary.

In fact, the situation is not so simple. As several scholars have pointed out—most recently, Raymond E. Brown[5]—there are good grounds for believing that the Virgin Birth (or virginal *conception*, as we should call it) was known and accepted as part of the teaching about Jesus in the apostolic period. There appear to be references to it in other Gospels and the Epistles,[6] and Mark's description of Jesus as 'the Son of Mary' [7] is highly significant—Jews were described as the sons of their fathers, not mothers . . . assuming that there *was* a father, that is. And undoubtedly there was an early Jewish slander about Jesus being illegitimate,[8] which suggests that the circumstances of his birth were not normal, at the very least.

Again, the virginal conception is most clearly related by Luke, the historian of the Evangelists, in a Gospel compiled, very probably, during or just after the end of the life-time of Mary. It seems impossible that the early Church could have accepted as fact something that she knew was not a fact. And it does seem that they accepted it as fact, not parable, allegory or midrash.

For the rest of the New Testament, with the obvious exception of the Revelation, we may be pretty confident about the literary form with which we are faced. Luke and Mark are clearly concerned to present biographies of Jesus in something fairly near the modern meaning of the word. Matthew and John are equally clearly writing theological

---

[5] *The Virginal Conception and Bodily Resurrection* by Geoffrey Chapman.

[6] e.g. John 1:13; Galatians 4:4

[7] Mark 6:3

[8] John 8:41

'interpretations' of the life and teaching of Jesus—Matthew's, with heavy rabbinical overtones. In Acts, we are back into straight-forward history, much of it verifiable from other records. The Epistles—most of them written before the earliest Gospels—are, of course, intended to explain, apply and defend the apostolic message, and strengthen the infant Church.

So it is not true, as some have claimed, that the new approach to hermeneutics demands that every Bible reader should first equip himself with a degree in biblical theology. It simply means that, if he wants to understand the Scriptures properly, he will expect to do some preparatory thinking, and reading, before approaching them. The 'simple' reader may approach the Bible 'simply' and it will accurately and with authority convey to him all that is necessary for salvation. The more sophisticated reader—the person who comes to the Bible with the cultural and intellectual conditioning of the modern world and therefore finds it strange and incredible—should be asked to pay this greatest of all books the compliment of approaching it with the care, preparation and awareness that he would bring to the plays of Aeschylus or the saga of Beowulf. Only then will he be released from the preconceptions that create most of his problems about the Bible, and in many cases create quite unnecessary tensions and contradictions.

7: WHAT ABOUT QUIRINIUS?

Hard cases make bad law, they say. But hard cases cannot be ignored, and in this chapter I want to sum up the case against literalism by taking two very difficult instances, one from the Old and the other from the New Testament, where a commitment to the literal accuracy of the Bible may put anyone's faith under terrible strain. Dr Francis Schaeffer, whom I instanced earlier as one of the doughtiest defenders of the literal school of thought, has gone on record as saying that it is *essential* for the truth of Christianity that the Bible should relate 'true truth' about 'history and the cosmos', as well as about spiritual matters. That is precisely the kind of claim that worries me, because it means that should any part of the Bible be shown to be inaccurate about 'history and the cosmos' then an essential part of the faith has gone. It seems to suggest that the alternatives before us are either the total and literal truth of everything the Bible says about 'history and the cosmos', or unbelief. In that case, for many people the only honest and consistent path would be to choose unbelief.

The two instances I have in mind are complete opposites

in almost every way. The first is the story of the creation of woman, in Genesis. Taken literally, it presupposes that the male element in human beings precedes the female element. Now that, according to Francis Schaeffer, must be part of 'true truth' about 'history and the cosmos'.

Recent research has suggested, however, that the human embryo is initially female, and that its male elements develop in response to a chemical 'trigger', testosterone: almost the precise opposite of the process described in Genesis.

Now this theory about human sexual origins may or may not eventually be disproven. For me, it is enough to postulate that at some future date it could be proven beyond any doubt. What would happen then to the young Christian who had hitched his wagon of faith to the literalist star? Where would that 'true truth' about the cosmos be? And the truly galling thing is that this predicament is totally unnecessary. All the pain, tension and damaged faith would have resulted from a non-existent conflict between 'faith' and 'science'.

Now let us turn to the other example, the governor Quirinius. Luke mentions, in passing, that the enrolment which brought Joseph and Mary to Bethlehem happened 'when Quirinius was governor of Syria'. I do not want to go into all the enormous wealth of historical analysis which has been lavished upon this statement over the years, and I am certainly not competent to judge between the various linguistic and historical theories that have been invoked to save Luke's reputation as an historian. What is quite obvious is that by any normal criteria Luke made a mistake.

The dates of the governorship of Quirinius are known from sound extra-biblical sources, including a carved inscription, and they do not coincide with the known dates of Herod, or of the enrolment in question.

From Egyptian papyri we know that enrolments like the

67

one that took Joseph and Mary to Bethlehem seem to have occurred once every fourteen years. There was certainly such a census in Judaea during the years AD 6–9 (it is referred to by Luke in Acts[1]), and we know that Quirinius became governor of Syria in AD 6. But that could not possibly have been the enrolment that coincided with the birth of Jesus, because it puts his date of birth too late to coincide with other historical reference points,[2] and also, as I have said, it would not have been during the reign of Herod the Great, who died in 4 BC. In the period during which Jesus must have been born, BC 9–4, the governors of Syria were Saturninus and Varus.

There would certainly have been a census, or enrolment, during the period BC 8–5, and as that coincides with the reign of Herod we may safely assume that the birth of Jesus occurred during those years.

But where does that leave Quirinius? The most obvious (though not for that reason necessarily the most convincing) explanation for Luke's reference to him is that he knew that Jesus was born during an enrolment, but confused the enrolment under Quirinius with the one that occurred fourteen years earlier.

Now it may be, of course, that Luke was absolutely accurate and that we lack some item of information, some missing piece in the jigsaw, which would vindicate his statement historically.[3] But supposing—as seems probable—Luke simply made a mistake: not a mistake over a matter of doctrine, faith, morals or behaviour, but over a completely unimportant detail of history concerning an obscure gover-

[1] Acts 5:37
[2] e.g. the dates of Pilate, AD 26–36
[3] For instance, the Lapis Tibertinus records the career of a Roman entering the office of legate 'for the second time'—and that might be Quirinius.

nor of a minor province two thousand years ago. Should my faith in the inspiration of the Bible, or, worse, my faith in Christ himself, be threatened by that? It would be, fatally, if I had to believe that the Bible conveys 'true truth' about '*history* and the cosmos' or in a word-for-word (verbal) doctrine of inspiration. That seems to me a perverse and essentially irrational stance to adopt, and one that creates a destructive and unnecessary confrontation.

Does it matter—in any ultimate meaning of the word 'matter'—whether Quirinius was or was not governor when Joseph and Mary went to Bethlehem? Of course it 'matters' whether Luke was an accurate historian, but is his reliability really at stake over so trivial a detail? Of course, many would invoke a domino theory here: if Luke is proven to be wrong over Quirinius, then he may be wrong over Bethlehem, and Joseph, and Mary, and John the Baptist, and a whole line of biblical 'dominoes' falls down.

But this, too, is a perverse argument. There might be a hundred reasons for Luke's mistake (if mistake it be) over Quirinius. Records available to him might themselves have been inaccurate. He might have confused two similar names, or miscalculated a sequence of dates. The whole thing might be an error by a later copyist or editor, or even by Luke's amanuensis. No historian has been immune from such things.

Equally, in any reasonable doctrine of inspiration, it is hard to insist that the Holy Spirit should give a cast-iron guarantee of historical accuracy where it is irrelevant to truth, doctrine or morals. St Paul, in his definitive statement on biblical inspiration, limits it not in terms of facts but of aims: 'All Scripture is inspired by God and is profitable for teaching the truth and refuting error, or for reformation of manners and discipline in right living.' Scripture is inspired in what it teaches and in the moral and spiritual standards

69

that it sets. There is no word here of an inspired guide to accurate information about 'history and the cosmos'. Within St Paul's definition, the matter of the dates of Quirinius is not within the aims of the inspiration of Scripture, whereas the doctrine of the incarnation clearly is. The one is not equally important with the other, and a doctrine of Scripture that would elevate the dates of Quirinius to a parity of importance with the nature of the Christ is obviously wrong-headed.

That is not to say, however, that the dates of Quirinius do not pose a problem. I have argued all along that the basic question in biblical interpretation is, what did the original writer intend? By that criterion, the creation of Eve creates no problem, because it is obvious that the writer was not giving a scientific or biological explanation of the origin of femaleness, but a theological explanation of the roles of the two sexes in the human race. But it is equally obvious that in the opening sentences of Luke's Gospel, chapter two, the writer is intending to write *history*, and so, by normal canons of interpretation, we should assess what he writes by historical criteria. And by those criteria, Luke is revealed as fallible, albeit over a very tiny detail, if he is mistaken over the dates of Quirinius.

So this passing reference, a mere parenthesis, does in fact represent something of a dilemma. We may let it stand for every other place in the historical sections of the Bible where there appear to be inaccuracies of detail, whether place-names, sizes of armies, identification of individuals or dates.[4] The Bible's history has been shown, by much painstaking research, to be remarkably reliable by the standards of comparable ancient records, but, not surprisingly, there are

[4] A clear-cut example from the Gospels is Mark 2:26: '. . . when Abiathar was high priest.' The high priest at the time in question was in fact Ahimelech.

a number of instances over matters of this kind where there is clearly some inconsistency or error of detail. How does this square with the principle of biblical inspiration? And how do we reconcile the apparent conflict between interpreting a passage in the light of the writer's intention and these instances where *even in those terms* the biblical text falls short of 'infallibility'?

It is that subject, and especially the emotive and potentially misleading word 'infallible', which we shall consider in the next chapter.

8: IS THE BIBLE 'INFALLIBLE'?

Although the word 'infallible' has been attached to the Bible by various groups and sects, especially in the last hundred years, it is not really a very helpful word to use about it. 'Infallible', in its dictionary meaning, describes something or someone that is incapable of erring, and while human beings have always longed for an infallible voice to show them the way, settle their disputes, and lead them into certainty, history only records the fallibility of every mouth and every mind that has claimed to do it.

God is by definition infallible, incapable of erring. If he were not, then he would not be God at all. If we believe in the divinity of Christ, then by analogy he too is infallible, though the doctrine of the incarnation obviously complicates that apparently simple statement. Clearly when Christ was on earth he was in some respects limited by his humanity—he could not be in two places at once, and his knowledge of affairs beyond our dimensions of time and space also appears to have been curtailed, probably voluntarily and temporarily.[1]

[1] See, for example, Matthew 24:36

Beyond that, it would seem there is simply no such thing as infallibility, in the strictly literal sense. We have seen that the Bible is not (and does not claim to be) an infallible guide to history, or science; and the doctrine of an 'infallible' Pope, to which, in popular thought, the Roman Catholic Church committed itself a century ago, is in fact nothing of the kind. It is so hedged around by conditions, limitations and qualifications that in practice it does not even approximate to the dictionary definition.

But that does not stop some people demanding infallibility. Indeed, some of the more fundamentalist missionary societies, Bible colleges and associations include the word in their 'bases of faith', and reject from membership those who do not subscribe to what is called the 'infallibility' of Scripture. Sometimes, as though that were not enough, the screw is turned a little tighter, and *verbal* infallibility or inerrancy are added to the qualities of the Bible. Others, perhaps trying to be helpful, turn the screw the other way, and limit the infallibility or inerrancy of the Bible to the texts 'as orginally given', though what practical value there is in believing in the infallibility of documents we no longer have it is hard to see.

However, for the most part 'infallibility' is a word that orthodox Christians have preferred not to use about the Scriptures, mainly because it claims more than the Bible claims for itself, and implies an almost magical omniscience for it about matters outside the limits of its inspiration. Yet some word is needed to describe the qualities of Scripture which make it unique.

Obviously 'inspired' is one—that is to say, inspired by the Holy Spirit. That is common ground to all Christians. The Scriptures, in St Paul's phrase, are 'God-breathed' [2]—not

[2] 2 Timothy 3:16, literally

brought about by human invention but by divine revelation through human instruments.

But 'inspiration' has lost some of its unique qualities as a word. When even a pop-song, or a concert performance, or a cover-drive at cricket can be called 'inspired', it is no wonder that Christians have looked for other words to express the unique nature of the Scriptures. Among the ones that have been most used are 'reliable' and 'authoritative'. The National Evangelical Anglican Congress at Nottingham in 1977—echoing the prestigious Lausanne Declaration of world-wide evangelicalism—spoke of the Bible as *reliable* in all that it genuinely affirms, and *authoritative* for guidance in doctrine and behaviour'. The Second Vatican Council, asserting that the biblical books were written under the inspiration of the Holy Spirit, saw them as teaching 'firmly, faithfully and without error that truth which God wanted put into the sacred writings for the sake of our salvation'. And this is no new, modern idea. The 'Thirty-nine Articles' of the Church of England, dating from the Reformation, make the same emphasis: 'Holy Scripture containeth all things necessary to salvation . . .'

These statements seem to me to express a biblical doctrine of the Bible, if I may be pardoned the tautology. They do not claim for it more than it claims for itself, but they stress positively and unambiguously exactly what it does claim: that when the Scriptures speak of doctrine, behaviour and the truths of salvation they do so reliably, authoritatively and without error. That is a true doctrine of 'infallibility'— an infallibility that guarantees truth where we need it, in the heart of the matter, where God reveals ultimate truth about himself, about ourselves and about the meaning and purpose of our existence.

It may be worth spending some time looking more closely at the relationship between inspiration and infallibility, because a number of red herrings habitually lurk in these waters and lure the unwary astray. For instance, I have said that by definition God is infallible; and it is part of the Christian 'case' that the Scriptures are inspired by God. Indeed, in times past many regarded the Bible as literally dictated by God, with the human writers merely transferring his words to paper (or parchment!). The Council of Trent in 1546 described the apostolic writings in the New Testament as produced 'at the dictation of the Holy Spirit', and many modern fundamentalists describe the process of the writing of Scripture in similar language.

Now, if the Scriptures are 'dictated'—or, if we reject that word, verbally inspired—by an infallible Author, should not they be regarded as infallible? And if we reject the infallibility of what the Reformers called 'God's Word written', are we not in fact blasphemously rejecting the infallibility of God?

This objection is irrefutable, it seems to me, if one accepts the 'dictation' theory of Holy Scripture. Clearly if God dictated the words, they are infallible, in every sense of the word.

But there are two problems here. The first is the manifest existence of errors of fact and detail in the Bible, not all of them capable of being explained as copyists' mistakes. I am thinking here of plain contradictions between different accounts of the same event: both cannot be right.[3] This would suggest either that God is *not* infallible, which is unthinkable; or that he did not dictate the words.

The second possibility is enhanced when we consider the problem of the human authors of the Bible. Dictation conveys the words of the dictator to paper. It carries his ideas in his idiom and style and vocabulary. But the biblical writings manifest scores of *different* idioms and styles, several different languages, and widely different choices of

[3] See, for example Matthew 27:3-7 and Acts 1:18,19

75

vocabulary. Not only that, but the revelation they give is progressive—the picture of God develops, changes, sharpens. The picture of God in Genesis is different from, though not a contradiction of, the picture of God in the Gospels.

But if God is dictating the words, why should he deliberately withhold part of the truth about himself from some of the writers? Why did he not give the writers of Genesis as complete a picture of himself as he gave St Paul or the seer of Revelation?

The answer is, of course, that the biblical writers are not mere typewriters, transferring God's words to paper. They are *writers*, in every sense of the word, with distinctive interests and insights, style, vocabulary and cultural conditioning. They wrote in the idiom of their day, using the images and figures of speech with which they were familiar. Even a casual reading of, say, Job, Luke and Daniel will reveal this kind of difference. '*Men they were*, but moved by the Holy Spirit, they wrote the words of God'[4]—fallible human beings were prompted by the Spirit to write what God wanted to say, to convey, very often, truths they themselves saw only dimly or partially. Taken together, put in their historical sequence, and rightly understood, the writers of the biblical books conveyed the Word of God. Through their human words, divine truth was revealed; God expressed himself.

It should not be too difficult for people who believe in the incarnation to grasp the paradox involved here. In Jesus, the God who inhabits eternity expressed himself in a human person. Of course, Jesus of Nazareth could not convey in himself certain truths about God—his omnipresence, for instance, or his eternity. His humanity limited him to one place at a time, and decreed that he should be born at Bethlehem and die on Calvary. Yet in a genuinely human

[4] 2 Peter 1:21

76

person God was present. Jesus looked like a first-century Jew, talked like one, used the idioms and vocabulary of his day. He was wholly and truly a man, though sinless. And yet we believe that through him God expressed himself adequately and effectively.

Jesus was the Word made flesh. The Scriptures are the Word made words. But just as being the Word of God did not mean that Jesus was not in every external aspect a first-century Jew, so writing the Word of God does not mean for the authors that they are not 'men of their time'. They were wholly and truly human—sinful, fallible, prejudiced, proud. Yet through them God expressed himself. 'Firmly, faithfully, and without error,' they wrote the Word of God, every truth which God wanted us to know.

For that purpose, it was not necessary for God to override their human limitations. Indeed, it would have been counter-productive. Their humanity was a vital link in the chain of revelation. It was an advantage, not a handicap.

The blazing and mysterious truth of God is literally incomprehensible to the human mind: 'My thoughts are not your thoughts,' says the Lord. But the biblical writers are recording and reflecting that same truth as human beings have experienced it—in their history, in their poetry, in story and allegory and vision. The Bible is God through human eyes: that is its strength and its glory. Just as Jesus makes the idea of God accessible by revealing him in human form, so the Scriptures make the truth of God accessible by revealing it in human ideas. And in the same way as Jesus was 'limited' by the incarnation, so the written Word is 'limited' by its human authorship.

Jesus was, in Charles Wesley's phrase, 'our God contracted to a span'. The Scripture is the truth of God 'contracted' to human size, not the truth as we shall one day know it ('then shall I know as I am known') but the truth as we can now comprehend it. The Bible does not tell us all there is to know about God, but it does tell us all we *need* to know about him: 'that truth which God wanted put into the sacred writings for the sake of our salvation'.

Within that limitation, it is permissible to speak of the inerrancy, or even infallibility, of Scripture. Scripture is 'reliable in all that it genuinely affirms'. It teaches 'firmly, faithfully and without error' the truth necessary for our salvation. In other words, inerrancy or infallibility is defined by the *end*, not the means. When the Bible affirms something, states that it is true and to be believed, it is infallible. When the Bible speaks of matters relating to our salvation, it is wholly reliable, it is infallible.

It could not really be otherwise. If God has chosen to reveal himself to man through a written Word, then the revelation of him which it gives must be trustworthy. What possible value would there be in a fallible, unreliable, untrustworthy revelation? We have plenty of those already. Jesus gave to the Old Testament Scriptures an irrefutable authority—'the Scriptures cannot be broken'. This does not mean, as some seem to suggest, that he was endorsing the historicity of Jonah or the cosmology of Genesis: what one wit has called 'the credibility of Eden and the edibility of Jonah'. His words are carefully chosen: the Scripture has supreme *authority*. It cannot be broken, set aside, ignored, contradicted. It is authoritative and trustworthy in what it affirms.

Similarly he gave to those who were to write, or compile, or provide the substance of the New Testament, a mandate to do it. The Holy Spirit would bring to their minds everything he had taught, so that what he said and did would be recorded accurately and authoritatively for those who were to come later.[5] Again there is no promise of historical

5 John 14:26

78

infallibility. The Holy Spirit would guarantee that what was recorded was what Jesus taught, or what God wanted to say to us through Jesus, presumably both in words and deeds. That can be received and believed as part of what 'God wanted to put into the sacred writings for the sake of our salvation'. Again, what use would a fallible, unreliable, untrustworthy record of Jesus be to us? We should be left, as are some of those who have rejected the New Testament's authority, to devise our own Christs, each one shaped to our own prejudices and preconceived philosophies. And we have enough of those already, too.

One doubt that may trouble the reader of the New Testament has been brought to the fore by modern biblical studies, and that is the alleged colouring of its reporting of events by the beliefs of the writers. For instance, it is commonly argued nowadays that the Gospels are records of the life of Jesus coloured by the compilers' belief in the resurrection. Indeed, the Fourth Gospel is seen as a picture not of Jesus as he was, but of Jesus as Christians of the second and third generation had come to regard him—a divine figure surrounded all the while by the after-glow of heaven, which he had recently left and to which he would shortly return. This divine Jesus, so the argument goes, is simply a projection back on to the traditional Gospel material of beliefs that had now come to be widely held in the Church.

Now this is not as negative a view as it might at first seem. Of course, knowledge gained at a later date colours our interpretation of past events. If I were to write a biography of Margaret Thatcher now, after she has become the first woman Premier in the western world, it would obviously be different from a biography written when she was an obscure but promising member of the parliamentary opposition. Naturally I would now interpret various incidents from the

79

past in a different way, seeing them as preparing her for high office, or, perhaps, as planned steps by her towards what was her lifelong ambition. Things do look different from different perspectives, and in that sense 'objectivity' is an empty word.

The Gospels were written long after the resurrection of Jesus. That is a fact. Even the oral tradition—the sayings of Jesus recounted in the early Church—came into existence in a community which was based on the belief that Jesus had risen from the dead. Naturally enough even the apostles, recalling the things Jesus had said and done, would have filtered them through their subsequent knowledge that he rose. Apparently innocuous statements—'Destroy this temple, and I will rebuild it in three days'—would be vested with a whole new significance in the light of later events.

But that is *not* distortion. An important ingredient in their understanding of Jesus, both as a person and as the Messiah, was missing until he had risen. Then the apostles could see the meaning in much of what he had said, and also implications in miracles and parables that simply would not have made sense when they first witnessed them. It is this knowledge that occasionally leads the Gospel writers to editorialise ('He said this because . . . he meant by this . . . they understood what this meant after Jesus was risen from the dead.'[6]). They were as aware as are our modern commentators that they were applying hindsight. They were also aware that to have excluded the devastating impact of the resurrection from their assessment of Jesus would indeed have been a distortion.

John's Gospel is, of course, rather special in this respect. It is very different from the others, not only in content— only one miracle, the feeding of the five thousand, is common to all four books—but also in style. The Jesus of

[6] See, for example, John 13:11 and John 2:22

the Fourth Gospel does not sound much like the Jesus of the Sermon on the Mount. He speaks in mysteries and weaves wonderful, mystical sermons around images like the vine, or bread, or sheep. He lifts his hearers up to heaven, and is overheard communing with his Father in terms of intimacy and equality. The plain-talking rabbi of the other Gospels, with his homely stories and blunt moral and ethical sayings, is conspicuously absent.

Does this mean, as some have claimed, that John's Gospel is useless as an historical portrait of Jesus of Nazareth, and of value only as a record of what the Church came to believe about him some five decades or more after the event? Does this also mean that all those profound and inspiring sayings of Jesus recorded in the Fourth Gospel are not authentic? What should we make of 'God so loved the world' and 'Let not your hearts be troubled . . . in my Father's house are many dwelling-places . . .' and 'I am the way, the truth and the life'? Are these to be seen simply as later interpolations, not based at all on the actual sayings of Jesus?

Before we abandon this part of our heritage as Christians, there are a few factors to be considered. For instance, the late dating of John's Gospel, for so long accepted as proven by the scholars, has been powerfully challenged by one of Britain's foremost New Testament scholars, Dr John Robinson.[7] He argues for a date before the fall of Jerusalem—in other words, within three decades of the crucifixion, at the latest. This puts the Fourth Gospel on a par with the others.

Even if Robinson is wrong, and this Gospel was written at the end of the first century or later, there would only be a case for arguing that it advances a 'new' and post-apostolic picture of Jesus if it is found to be advancing ideas and doctrines not present in the earliest documents about him. But the earliest documents, by common consent, are not the

[7] In *Redating the New Testament* (SCM)

first three Gospels, but some of the letters of St Paul. And the picture that emerges of the teaching of Jesus from those letters is actually closer to that recorded in John's Gospel than the others. Paul's Christianity is rooted in the divinity of Jesus, in the Word made flesh, in the mystic unity between Christ and the believer, in the life of the divine Son of God sacrificed on the Cross and accepted by the Father. All the themes of the Fourth Gospel are present in St Paul, even in the earliest letters, which suggests that this is no alien or 'other' Gospel, but the heart of the matter, the *meaning* (in the profoundest sense) of the incarnation.

Which brings us back to the question of inspiration and inerrancy. If the intention of John (or whoever compiled his recollections of Jesus) and Paul was to interpret and apply the authentic message of Christ, then the principle of inspiration which we have established would ensure that what they wrote conveyed that message 'firmly, faithfully and without error'. The principle does not guarantee the quasi-historical details in the Fourth Gospel (including the sequence of events) nor does it help us distinguish between the actual words of Jesus and John's interpretation of them. For instance, no one really knows, in that fascinating discourse between Jesus and Nicodemus, where the reply of Jesus ends and John's commentary on it begins.

Nor does it really matter, for *both* are covered by an inspiration which applies to the end product, the 'truth which God wanted put' there.

With regard to what I called the 'quasi-historical details' of the Fourth Gospel, an important distinction should be made between history that conveys spiritual truth, and history that is irrelevant to it. This doctrine of inerrancy requires that if an historical event is part of the truth God wants to convey in the Scripture, then it must be accurately recorded. The crucifixion and resurrection of Jesus and his ascension to the Father clearly fall in this category, because they guarantee doctrines of the faith which are central to our salvation.

At the other extreme, the dates of Quirinius, or the identity of the high priest at the time of the trial of Jesus, or the details of the way the body of Jesus was prepared for burial—all of which are matters of historical controversy— are clearly not covered by this doctrine of inerrancy. No doctrine of salvation is attached to them. No great truth stands or falls with them.

As usual in such arguments, however, there are the border-line cases, where the principle does not seem to apply. For instance, the resurrection of Jesus (as I have said) is a central truth of salvation. Therefore, by this doctrine of inspiration, we should expect the Gospel accounts of it to be historically reliable. If, as St Paul claims, faith itself stands or falls by the truth of the resurrection, we may reasonably ask for reliable and authoritative accounts of it in the Gospels.

But in fact, as a careful reading of the Gospels will reveal, we are faced with a number of apparently irreconcilable contradictions in these accounts. It is not possible, without deciding to favour one account rather than another, to establish how many angels appeared at the tomb, what they said or who of several different witnesses was actually the first to get there. Was the body of Jesus bound up (as John claims) 'after the burial customs of the Jews' or wrapped in a simple shroud, as the other Gospels claim? Was it embalmed before the Sabbath or did the women come to the tomb on the Sunday expecting to do this last service for their Master? None of these details is clear.

What is clear, however, is that *taken together* the four accounts of the resurrection create a most convincing body of evidence, made all the more authentic by the obvious absence of collusion between the witnesses. Taken overall, they tell the same story, from different angles and perspectives, agreeing over every important fact and only disagreeing, or appearing to disagree, over secondary details. The inspiration of the Holy Spirit has not eliminated these human differences. He has let the witnesses speak for themselves. But overall he has presented us with one of the best attested accounts in ancient history. The truth that Jesus rose emerges with triumphant clarity, reinforced rather than weakened by the independence of the witnesses.

This chapter is headed, 'Is the Bible infallible?' On the whole, as I have suggested, that is probably not the right question to ask, because it carries overtones of literal, scientific or historical accuracy that are irrelevant to its chief purpose, to make known the saving truth of God. Nevertheless, within the limits Scripture sets for itself, we can indeed describe it as 'infallible'—incapable of error. Rightly understood, rightly interpreted and rightly applied, it is 'infallible' where it matters, teaching 'firmly, faithfully and without error' the truth which it sets out to convey, teaching us reliably all we need to know for our salvation.

9: WHAT ABOUT THE MIRACLES?

There is little doubt in my mind that at the heart of all the recent scholarly debate about the person of Jesus, and the re-interpretation of the Gospels, lies a fundamental disagreement about the supernatural. On the one side are those who believe in miracles, in a God who 'intervenes' in human and natural affairs. On the other side are those who reject any supernatural explanation of events, and who believe in a God who is present in what he has made but does not interfere with the normal and natural course of things. The first group finds no difficulty in accepting the divinity of Christ, and with it the full picture of Jesus presented by the Gospels, including the Fourth. The second group has difficulty over accepting the divinity of Christ, at any rate in any orthodox sense, and regards the portrait of Jesus in the Gospels—and especially the Fourth—as heavily influenced by later accretions.

In other words, beliefs about the nature of the Gospels follow on from beliefs about the person of Christ, which in turn follow on from beliefs about the nature of God. Of course the argument is seldom presented in that way. It always seems as though the protagonists are starting from an examination of the Gospels. But they bring to that examination (as we all do) various preconceptions, and among them will necessarily be an attitude towards the miraculous or supernatural.

Now those who approach the Gospels with the preconceived idea that anything miraculous or supernatural in them must have come from later accretions, reflecting the beliefs of a Christian community that saw Jesus as a divine visitor from the other world, will obviously find much of the material unconvincing. From their basic assumptions they must reject the greater part of the narratives, and assume that only the teaching is authentic.

For them, God does not 'intervene', and to talk of his 'breaking through into the human world' in Jesus is a nonsense. He is there already, and all that Jesus did was to focus in himself that ever-present divinity. Far from 'taking our nature upon him', Jesus the man simply opened himself to God and revealed in a human life his grace, his love and his compassion. He did not bring heaven to earth, because it is there—potentially at least—already. God did not 'invade' planet earth, because he had never been away.

There is a great deal that is true in this way of looking at the incarnation, and it certainly helps to counteract some of the more extreme and sensational versions that have crept into devotional writing and preaching from time to time, mine included. The idea of God invading this planet in Jesus, for instance, is a very unhelpful and potentially misleading one, suggesting as it does that he had hitherto been absent from it. Again, the idea of Jesus as a kind of divine superman from space paying us a brief visit is a travesty of the biblical doctrine of the incarnation. And indeed the whole notion of divine 'intervention', while not as foreign to the biblical view of God as its critics would suggest, does convey overtones of dualism, as though in some way the One who created and now sustains the universe has lost control of it, apart from occasional supernatural forays.

The weakness of this view, it seems to me, is that it skirts a great deal of inconvenient biblical evidence, and also ignores the doctrine of the Fall.

While it is true that God is ever-present in his world, it is equally true that at specific times the Bible claims that he has been visibly active in people and events. The exodus from Egypt has always been seen by the Jews as an action of God in time and space, intended to alter the apparently inevitable course of history and bring Israel out of captivity into a new and special relationship with him. This is not to say that God had not been 'with' them before, or that he left them after their arrival in this promised land. But it does presuppose a deliberate divine action of an extraordinary kind, and it is hard to believe that anyone reading the Bible with an unprejudiced eye would deny that from time to time these extraordinary actions are recorded. They were not, in general, such as to overthrow natural law, but to concentrate the ever-present power of God in bringing about his will in history.

The 'Fall' is central to any adequate understanding of the Bible. It is an explanation of an observable phenomenon, that while this is a 'good earth', and human beings reflect many of the attributes of their Creator, yet at the heart of things there is a moral flaw, a corruption. There is love and caring, but there is also hatred, cruelty and injustice. There is beauty, but there is also ugliness. There is generosity and charity, but there is also greed and exploitation. The Christian explanation is simple but stark: man was created good, but a free moral agent, and by his own choice has declined to obey God and instead pursued his own ends. As a result, the image of God in man has been defaced. He looks like an angel, but very often behaves like a devil.

Consequently, the world which God created, and over which he still has ultimate authority, is in a state of rebellion against him. The human race has exercised its moral freedom to reject God's way and go its own.

God's answer to this is not simply to allow the state of affairs to continue, but to intervene (it is hard to think of another word) to re-assert his claims on mankind, to demonstrate his love for them and provide through his Son Jesus a 'way back'. Hence St Paul's vivid title for Christ, the 'second Adam'—the one who made it possible for mankind to reverse the disaster of the Fall and once again be at one with their Creator.

Now this action of God cannot be dismissed as simply a manifestation of his immanence, his presence in every part of his creation. That does not do any kind of justice to the language the New Testament uses about the incarnation. However we interpret it, there can be no denying that St Paul, and the writers of all four Gospels, saw Jesus as a representative of God, acting in the name of God in a way that no prophet of old, not even Moses, had done.

Part of that 'acting' involved the working of miracles— not only healing the sick, but casting out demons, multiplying bread and fish, and even raising the dead. The response of the 'naturalists' is to say that the miraculous element in the Gospel is a later addition, the ministry of Jesus seen through the eyes of men who already believed him to be divine.

This seems to fall into the same category as the critical response to the fulfilment of prophecy. If a prophecy of the Old Testament is said to have been fulfilled in Christ, then the action or event that demonstrates its fulfilment is a midrash *every time*. The critic has decided in advance that there is no such thing as a fulfilled prophecy (although, as we have seen in the instance of John the Baptist preceding Jesus, prophecy is sometimes demonstrably fulfilled). On the basis of that decision, however, *all* references to prophecy are judged.

Similarly, many critics have decided, for the reasons I set out earlier, that miracles do not happen. Consequently, every miraculous event, even the resurrection itself, is seen as a later interpolation. No matter how well attested by normal historical criteria, any event which has a supernatural explanation is to be rejected as inauthentic.

I remember producing a series of radio talks on the miracles of Jesus, several years ago. Among the contributors were the Methodist peer, Lord Soper, and the great Scottish biblical expositor, Dr William Barclay. Both were determined to reject the supernatural element in the Gospels, at any rate where physical events are concerned. But their approach was totally different. Dr Soper rationalised the miracles. The five thousand were persuaded by Jesus to share their lunches, so that all were fed. The vision of Jesus walking on the water was a misapprehension by the disciples—Jesus was in fact wading through ankle-deep shallows at the side of the lake. And so on.

Dr Barclay, on the other hand, spiritualised them. For him, every miracle was in the mind. When Jesus stood up in the storm-tossed boat and calmed the storm that had terrified his disciples, the miracle was not that the storm stopped but that he calmed the fear in their hearts. Indeed, Barclay claimed, it is a greater miracle to make a coward brave than to silence a tempest.

The significance of their different responses is largely a matter of history. Dr Soper's rationalism has the feel of an earlier age, when the biblical account was accepted but explained in ways that removed the supernatural. Dr Barclay reflects a newer approach. The miracles express truths about Jesus as the early Christians experienced him. He calmed their hearts. He fed their souls. He gave them new life. These experiences were fed back into the Gospel material in the form of miracle stories and took their place alongside the authentic rabbinical-style teaching of Jesus.

But in both cases the *a priori* assumption is that *miracles do not happen*. If they do, however rarely—if human history records any events which permit of no natural explanation— then surely we should expect them to happen in connection with this extraordinary action of God in Jesus. If there has ever been a miraculous healing, even once, then who is more likely to have done it than God's Son? It seems a special kind of intellectual arrogance to claim that nothing anywhere has ever happened that cannot be explained by the known laws of human science. It also seems intrinsically incapable of proof. That is a slender base on which to build so massive an edifice of scepticism about the Gospel miracles.

So I do not think we need feel impelled to go along with this scepticism. To rule out any possibility of the miraculous is, logically, to rule out the existence of God himself, because the idea of a first cause is in itself miraculous.

But this does not have to be a licence for credulity. Taking the history of Christendom as a whole credulity and super- stition have undoubtedly done as much damage to the Church as scepticism and doubt. The ludicrous 'miracles' of the Middle Ages, with saints' bones and fingernails healing the sick and even raising the dead, devalued the Gospel itself. It is interesting that both the Protestant Reformers and the Counter-Reformation played down the role of the miraculous, without, of course, ruling it out entirely. Sadly, today we seem to have a resurgence of a mindless credulity in Christendom, with books with titles like *Every moment a miracle* or *Expect Great Things* selling by the million and hundreds of fast-talking evangelists and spiritual healers cashing in on the boom.

In such a climate, one has to emphasise that miracles are *extraordinary* actions of God. By definition, if they occur daily—or even 'every moment'—they are not extraordinary, but commonplace. The perspective offered us by the 'naturalists', those who emphasise the immanence of God and his presence and activity in every part of his creation, may be a helpful counterbalance to this new fanaticism.

In fact, it is this balance between the transcendent God— God above and beyond us, altogether 'other' than we are, all-powerful and all-knowing—and the immanent God, who is ever-present within all that he has made, that is so crucial. Temperamentally and intellectually some of us are more inclined to a God 'above' (a miracle-working, intervening God) and some to a God 'within' (a God who works through nature and order, which are his creatures). The tension between the two need not be destructive, for both preserve vital truths about the nature of God. But the transcendentalist must not deny the God who is ever-present in his creation, and those who emphasise immanence must not deny God the right to act independently of the laws of nature if he wishes to. Both truths are present in Scripture, and complement each other. Indeed, neither can really make sense without the other.

The same balance should be struck in considering the role of the miraculous in the Bible. Some will look at the biblical miracles and see in them the way God is endlessly present and at work in nature and history, so that 'all that exists is alive with his life', as John's Gospel expresses it. Others will find in the same accounts a record of God, who is wholly 'other', at work in specific events to bring about his will. Neither view necessarily excludes the other, and both express a truth about God which is only distorted if either is completely denied.

But that is not to say that every account of a miracle in the Bible is to be treated in the same way. To argue that miracles *can* happen is not to say that they always *do* happen, or that every description of an extraordinary action of God in the Bible is to be taken literally.

The miracles of Christ undoubtedly fall in a class of their own, both in their restraint and in their significance. Unlike most of the Old Testament miracles, they were written up within the life-time of eye-witnesses, they took place in known and identified places and involved named people. They were not, for the most part, 'magical', but were expressions of loving concern, actions aimed at making people whole. And they are related in a calm, matter-of-fact way which is nearer to historical documentation than extravagant fiction.

In contrast, many of the Old Testament miracles have the flavour of the legendary saga about them. The mighty deeds of Samson, for instance, or the story of Jonah and the whale seem to fall in that category. The way they are related, the distance in time between the reported event and its incorporation into the written record, and the absence of reliable historical points of reference, have all been given as reasons for treating them as non-historical. But the important question when considering how we should interpret these stories is not 'Do we think it could have happened like that?' nor even 'What is the historical likelihood of this story being factual?' but the old and basic one, 'What did the writer intend?' With many of these saga-like narratives I have little doubt that the writer's primary concern was to illustrate the power or purpose of God rather than to document historical events.

When we turn to the Gospel miracles we are moving in a

different milieu. Here there is little or none of the magical element—axe-heads are not required to float, or donkeys to talk, or suns to move backwards in their orbits. The miracles of Jesus, for the most part, are miracles *with* nature rather than against it. Few today would dispute the spiritual element in healing, both of the mind and the body, where nature seems to be harnessed in a positive way and God-given spiritual resources in people are released and applied. But the same might be said to be true of other miracles. God multiplies bread and fish to feed mankind. Usually it takes months or even a year. At the hands of the Creator's Son it takes minutes. God turns the water in the soil into juice in the grape and wine in the barrel. The process takes months or years. In the hands of Jesus it takes a second or two. These miracles are not anti-nature, but are instances or pictures of the normal physical processes of creation being accelerated and concentrated.

I used the words 'instances or pictures' deliberately, for while personally I can accept these miracles of Jesus as historical (that is to say, I can believe that they happened substantially as the evangelists report them), I do not think any essential doctrine of inspiration is at stake if others see them as *pictures* rather than *instances*. Although I think it is straining the interpretation of the writers' intentions, I could not say that it is impossible that they were intending in these stories to make profound 'preaching points' about Jesus rather than to describe actual events. Jesus feeds us and satisfies us; Jesus turns the water of the world into the rich, red wine of the kingdom. For myself, these miracles speak more clearly if they are seen as records of what he did, rather than what he meant, like the acted parables of the prophets.[1] But it is emphatically the meaning that matters.

[1] See, for instance, Jeremiah 13:1–11

In any case, there is only one absolutely crucial miracle in the New Testament—beyond the incarnation itself—and that is the resurrection of Jesus. Once we can accept that, all the others assume a different perspective. Conversely, if we cannot accept it, then it is hard to see how we can be called 'Christians' at all. The first Christians were people who believed in the resurrection. Without that faith, there was nothing.[2] It was the resurrection that was the basis of the apostles' preaching, and upon that foundation the Church itself was built—a community of people who believed that Jesus of Nazareth was alive and that they had 'met' him.

The common experience of the early Christians was of this meeting with the risen Christ. Not all met him as dramatically as Paul did on the Damascus Road, but every one of them could speak of 'knowing Christ' or 'receiving Christ' or 'living in Christ'—and they were not talking about a dead leader. For them, this was the transforming truth, the difference between defeat and victory, between despair and triumph. It is impossible to understand the early Church without grasping the centrality of the resurrection.

Naturally, so powerful an experience influenced everything the apostolic Church said or did. Of course it affected their understanding of the Gospel stories, of the sayings of Jesus, of Old Testament prophecies and even of the miracles. It was for them the vital element that made sense of everything else, and I think it is fair to say that in the last analysis only those who share their faith in the risen Christ can share their dynamic understanding of the Gospels. They did not arrive at their faith in Jesus through historical analysis, but through the infectious

[2] 1 Corinthians 15:14

awareness in the Christian community of his risen life. He validates the Gospels, not vice versa.

That is why the Church's role in our approach to the Scriptures is important. It is that role that we shall be looking at in the next chapter.

10: THE THREE-LEGGED STOOL

The Bible did not drop from heaven in one piece. While everybody knows that, many people speak about it as though it did. A verse from the Psalms is regarded in exactly the same way as a verse from the letter to the Ephesians. A statement by Jeremiah will be cross-referred to a statement by St Paul as though they were on a par, and not separated by centuries of history, vast changes in cultural environment, a different language and the intervention of the coming of the Messiah.

The Bible was written by scores of different authors over a period of perhaps a thousand years, and its final form, the Bible as we now have it, was not settled until the fifth century AD.

As we have seen already, the primary 'cause' of the Bible is the inspiration of the Holy Spirit. That is to say, the one common factor which distinguishes Holy Scripture from other writings is the Church's belief that it is divinely inspired. But someone has to decide what is and what is not inspired, and it is there that the role of the Church is so important. The canon of Scripture—the list of the books of the Old Testament—had been established among the Jews by the time of Jesus, but the decision to add to it the writings of the New Testament was one over which the early Church agonised. Clearly by the time of the second letter of Peter[1] the writings of St Paul were regarded as on a par with 'Scripture', by which is meant, of course, the Old Testament. But the decision as to which writings should be included was not an easy one.

Anyone even slightly familiar with the literature of the early Church will know that the Gospels and Epistles which are in our Bibles are paralleled by many similar writings. Some of these were highly regarded in the first centuries, and widely respected. Some undoubtedly recorded genuine sayings and actions of Jesus—the 'Gospel of Thomas', for instance. From this mass of material the 'New Testament' was chosen, though not without a good deal of argument and controversy.

The tests that were applied are interesting in a wider context. Obviously the Church Councils asked if the piece of writing under consideration was authentic, reliable and accurate. But the crucial test was whether it was 'apostolic', and by that they meant written by an apostle, or enshrining the teaching of an apostle. Modern textual scholarship suggests that few of the New Testament books were actually written by any of the apostles, in our technical sense of the word—they did not pen the words, nor, in some cases, literally dictate them. But there is plenty of evidence of apostolic authority, and obviously the Councils of the Church, meeting to consider the canon of Scripture, scrutinised the disputed books closely. They were nearer the originals than we are, and better placed to detect the authentic 'flavour' of the apostolic source, even if they

[1] 2 Peter 3:16

lacked the tools of linguistic and textual study which we have today.

Now these Councils were discussing an absolutely vital question. They were convened to decide which of a vast mass of early Christian writings were inspired by the Holy Spirit. As St Paul had pointed out in his letter to Corinth, only those who possess the Holy Spirit can recognise his work.[2] By this argument, the Councils which decided the canon must have been guided by the same Holy Spirit who had earlier guided the writers.

In other words, there is a double inspiration, of the writers (what we might call the primary inspiration) and of the Church's leaders who recognised it—a kind of secondary inspiration.

The astonishing thing over the subsequent centuries of dispute about almost everything else to do with Christian doctrine, is how little dispute there has been over their decisions. By and large history and scholarship have endorsed the work of the Councils. They rejected the dross—sometimes, very popular dross—and they recognised the genuine article.

This might appear to suggest that the Church is the primary authority, and the Scripture, which depends on it for authentication, is secondary. In fact, the issue is not quite so simple. The message of the Gospel—the *kerygma* in Greek—preceded the existence of the Church. Indeed, the Church came into being as a result of the *kerygma* being proclaimed. That message is like a living nucleus at the heart of the New Testament. The Gospels are accounts of and reflections on the message in the person of Jesus. The Acts is a report of the message proclaimed by the growing Church. The Epistles show us the message worked out in the life of the local churches. At the heart of it all is the

[2] 1 Corinthians 2:9–16

kerygma, and without it there would have been no Church at all.

But equally, without the Church there would have been no New Testament. The *kerygma* may be the nucleus, but the New Testament is more than that. It includes the *didache* (the 'teaching') of the Church, providing the Christian community then and to the present day with 'that truth which God wanted put into the sacred writings for the sake of our salvation'.

So it is futile to argue about the relative authority of the Bible and the Church. Ideally there is no conflict, and where it has arisen it is either because the Church has drifted away from the Bible or individualistic interpretations of the Bible have taken it away from the Church. The Church is built upon the Word. The Word is recognised by the Church. They are, or should be, absolutely inseparable.

This is an important factor in the interpretation of the Bible, for it should predispose the reader to interpret it as the Church has always done, rather than look for novel or revolutionary interpretations. Of course new insights do emerge—the Christian faith is not static—but it is absolutely right that they should be carefully and almost grudgingly accepted, only being endorsed by the Christian Church when it is clear that they are true to the spirit of the Scriptures and in line with the apostolic faith.

However, there is an authority that lies behind that of both the Bible and the Church, and that is the authority of Christ. As we saw earlier, he endorsed the authority of the Old Testament; he himself is the Gospel; and he authorised the apostles to record 'everything that he had taught them'. So his authority stretches back to the patriarchs and forward to the end of the apostolic writings. It embraces both the writings which he endorsed and the community which he founded.

Now clearly this could be considered a circular argument, because it is the Church that recognises the Bible, and the Bible that tells us the words of Christ—which, of course, authorise both the Bible and the Church. But instead of seeing this as a circular argument, we could see it as a three-legged base for a reliable doctrine of revelation: the Bible, the incarnation, and the Church. The incarnation was an event in time which brought the authority and truth of God into the human dimension. It is, for Christians, the decisive event in human history, and Jesus the apex of the revelation of God to mankind. The Bible sets the incarnation in its theological context—the Fall, the giving of the law, the calling out of Israel, the gathering momentum of longing for a Saviour.

It then gives us the only authoritative account of the event itself, what some scholars like to call the Christ-event. And finally it gives us the interpretation of that event from those who were the first to experience its dynamic impact.

The Church provides the third leg, for in the Christian community is given the only authentication of this that really counts, the experience of the living Christ, and his gift of the Holy Spirit. It was that that turned the first disciples from terrified adherents into exuberant witnesses. They knew the 'facts'—in the upper room they were given all the evidence they were ever to receive of the fact of the resurrection, and they were clear about the identity of Jesus the Messiah.[3] But it was not until the facts were fired with the resurrection faith, and the gift of the Holy Spirit, that the incarnation made its real impact on their lives.

These three 'legs'—Bible, incarnation and Church—are totally interdependent. Take one away and the 'chair' falls down. But it is more than that. Each authenticates the other,

[3] Luke 9:20

in such a way that it is futile to try to say that one is 'primary' and another 'secondary'.

For instance, the incarnation endorses the Old Testament and gives birth to the Church of the New Testament. But it is the Bible that provides us with our only record of the incarnation and most of our interpretation of it, and it is the Church that recognises and endorses the Bible.

We can see in the history of Christianity what happens when one or other of these 'legs' is undervalued. The sects that reject or dilute the divine Sonship of Jesus invariably misunderstand the rest of the Bible, too. Although accepting its inspiration and even infallibility, they do not see it through the perspective of the incarnation, and without that it is distorted. The Protestant churches after the Reformation in many cases undervalued the authority of the Church. The result was a riot of 'personal judgments' on the Bible with a proliferation of denominations and groups based upon different interpretations of details of the Scriptures, viewed, very often, apart from their historic setting in the bosom of the Church. At the other extreme, the medieval Church virtually ignored the Bible, and all manner of superstition, error and corruption was tolerated and even encouraged.

But to say that the Bible (the written Word), the incarnation (the Word made flesh) and the Church (the Word in action) are interdependent is not to say, of course, that they are equally authoritative where doctrine is concerned. Clearly the written record, which cannot be changed or corrupted by human error, is normative today. The Church cannot teach anything that is contrary to the written record that it has endorsed. To do so would in fact be to undermine or contradict its own authority.

When the three 'legs' are in their right places, the pattern of revelation emerges. It is faith in Christ, the incarnate Son of God, that is the key, giving meaning and purpose to the

Old Testament and his own authority to the New. And it is the Church, the community of the Holy Spirit, built upon the incarnation, that guards and guarantees the Scriptures, ensuring that they are not distorted, misinterpreted or emasculated. Over the centuries this has been the weakest 'leg', of course, as time and again the Church has *not* guarded the Scriptures. At times it has almost ignored them, and at other times it has stood by while their authority or authenticity has been undermined. But still it is the duty of the Christian community, and specifically of its leaders, to be the guardian of the faith, and it is still more likely to do it than any of the other contenders—exotic sects, individualistic commentators or self-appointed prophets.

Traditionally this guarding of the faith from error in the Church is the work of the bishop. Certainly one Anglican bishop, who was quite controversial in his theology before, told me that at the time of his consecration he decided that his days of questioning were over. From then on, he vowed, there would be no room in his public ministry for speculative theology. After all, he was now called to be a guardian of the faith, one who sets the limits rather than tests them.

Through all the vicissitudes of recent biblical confusion it is also a remarkable fact that the great Churches of Christendom have not allowed their official formularies to shift with each conflicting breath of fashion. When all the noise and confusion and smoke clears, we may well find that those formularies, understood in a dynamic way, are still the best guarantee we have that what the Church teaches is what Christ taught, and what we believe is what the apostles believed.

11: A DYNAMIC WORD

One of the recurrent ideas of the New Testament is that the Word of God is 'alive' or 'living' or 'active'.[1] Taken in their historical contexts, these references cannot literally be applied to the Bible on my bookshelf, because it did not then exist, and was not yet designated 'the Word of God'. What the New Testament writers were saying was that when God speaks, the 'words' he utters are dynamic. We can think of the creation story in Genesis. It was by the words of God, 'Let there be light', that the whole process of creation began. Since then, whenever God has spoken it has had an effect. What he says is not just information, comment or reflection. It is effective; it brings about an effect.

So while, as I say, this cannot be taken in a literal way to apply to the Bible on my bookshelf, it can by a logical development be taken to mean that as that Bible conveys to me the Word of God it becomes alive and has an effect upon me. The Bible is very much more than information, advice or comment—even inspired information, advice or comment. It is 'alive and active'—but only as I read it with faith. The book, the paper, the ink and the words themselves are simply the mechanics that make it possible for the living

[1] e.g. Hebrews 4:12, 1 Peter 1:23

Word of God to enter my mind and achieve there his intended effect.

For that reason, if for no other, we should beware of being too dogmatic about the interpretation of individual passages of Scripture. If it is 'alive' it can adapt, a basic quality of life. So I should not be surprised if a story or saying in the Bible (even out of context) speaks to me on a particular occasion with enormous relevance and impact, whereas on previous occasions when I have read it there has been no such effect. The words have not changed, but my situation has, and the 'living Word' is speaking to me out of the past into the present. Sometimes an allegorical interpretation lights up a familiar passage in a totally new way. Sometimes we bring a particular need to our reading and the 'Word' speaks to that need. And sometimes, released from the straightjacket of literalism, the Bible, which had previously seemed to us to be a static, historical document which we needed to defend and justify, becomes instead a book of blazing originality and profound revelation of truth *here and now*.

Some years ago a revered evangelical minister warned me against speaking of the 'inspiringness' of the Bible instead of its inspiration. He meant that it is inspired whether we find it inspiring or not, and I took his point. However, I would now want to say that an inspired book *should* be inspiring, and if we find the Bible boring, insipid or incredible the fault must lie in us, not in the concept of inspiration.

To me, the key words are faith and imagination. We must believe that the Bible is inspired by God, and then we must allow the Holy Spirit, who is its ultimate cause, to fire our imaginations so that we receive its full, dynamic impact. Of course, quite a large part of the Old Testament *is* boring— page after page of tribal lists or chronologies, or details of the building plans of the tabernacle. It is hard to regard it as inspiring, in any normal sense of the word, even though it has the *cachet* of being part of the inspired Scriptures. But, rightly understood and in their historical contexts, even apparently unpromising material can often 'speak' to us.

The danger is that we shall go fishing for 'meanings'. I recall a booklet of devotional Bible notes which suggested to its readers that as they ploughed their way through a chapter of the book of Numbers which consisted of nothing but a list of tribes and families, they might care to reflect that this teaches us how God cares for the individual!

Equally, as we saw earlier, an allegorical approach can lead to a situation in which we are squeezing out of the Bible things that the Holy Spirit did not put there. Sermons on David's 'five smooth stones' or Samson's foxes with flaming tails are seldom based on anything remotely connected with the intentions of the original writers. 'Imagination' does not, in this context, mean imagining something that simply is not there.

Let me illustrate what I mean about reading with faith and imagination by taking two miracles of Jesus and considering how a dynamic approach can give them a fresh meaning and impact.

Several times Jesus healed lepers. Let us take one instance, recorded by Luke in chapter 5. A man 'covered with leprosy' approached Jesus, bowing to the ground and begging for help. 'If only you will, Sir,' he said, 'you can cleanse me.'

Jesus stretched out his hand and touched him, saying, 'Indeed I will; be clean again.'

The leprosy left the man, and Jesus told him to show himself to the priest, and make the offering prescribed in the law, but not tell anyone else. In the event, the news was spread all over the district.

Now, that sounds a fairly run-of-the-mill Gospel miracle, if I may be forgiven the phrase. If it is simply taken as yet another demonstration of the power of Jesus to heal, it is hard to see why it is included in the New Testament—after all, one leper healed is much like another, and there are several other than this one described in the Gospels. I suspect that many a person taking the traditional, 'conservative' view of the Bible, would simply read it, silently note that it was yet another example of the miraculous power of Christ, and move on to the next passage. After all, if it is simply an historical account, that is about all there is to do with it. Faith, at least, is vindicated.

But imagination would add so much more. Obviously, if the Bible conveys the dynamic Word of God—a living, active, effective word—then this miracle is included in order to do more than simply catalogue another wonder. It must be (in Paul's words) of value in 'teaching the truth, refuting error, correcting behaviour or training us in right living.'

Let us imagine the process by which this story came to be in Luke's Gospel. Along with many other stories of the extraordinary acts of Jesus, it would undoubtedly have been part of the oral tradition which was passed on from church to church in the early years of Christianity. This was the 'resurrection community', of course—a community of people who believed that Jesus was the risen Son of God, the one who had come to fulfil all the prophecies and hopes of the Old Testament. As the stories of Jesus were related, we can visualise the preacher interpreting them, showing again and again how they filled out the truth they believed about Jesus, illustrating and endorsing his divine role as the servant, redeemer and king.

When he came to this one, he would hardly have failed to connect it with the Old Testament prophecies of a new source of cleansing.[2] Leprosy in Bible times (whatever its precise medical definition) was unquestionably a dreaded

[2] Zechariah 13:1

and contagious disease which disfigured, disabled and separated its victim from the rest of the community: a telling analogy of sin. The preacher would have drawn out the link with the Old Testament 'cleansing' through sacrifice, and also, probably, the role of faith ('If only you will, you can cleanse me') and submission to Jesus ('he bowed to the ground'). Perhaps he would also have noted that Jesus 'touched him'—identifying himself with the diseased body, willing if need be to take the dreaded infection upon himself: 'by his wounds you have been healed.'[3]

When the written Gospels came to be compiled, the selection of incidents to be recorded for posterity was based, I suggest, not simply on the answer to the question 'Did it happen?'—if it had been, we have John's assurance that the world would not have been big enough to contain them[4]— but on the answer to the question, 'What does it tell us about Jesus?' And especially, 'What does it tell us about Jesus that other stories do not?' By those criteria, this story of the cleansing of the leper took precedence over other miracles of healing. It became part of the sacred record, the adequate, reliable and authentic picture of Jesus which the Gospels, under the Holy Spirit, are to give us. And the crucial factor in its inclusion was its dynamic quality, its relevance to the Church.

But what about more contentious examples? Miracles of healing pose comparatively few problems, but the feeding of the five thousand is a different matter. It is obviously the kind of miracle that tests the credulity of the modern reader. How, he asks himself, did the alleged miracle occur? Did Jesus literally—magically, almost—multiply bread and fish, before the very eyes of the onlookers? And how would this happen—by new loaves appearing from nowhere, or broken

[3] I Peter 2:24
[4] John 21:25

pieces growing or multiplying? Or were minute crumbs given to each person present, but miraculously satisfied them? The difficulties are obvious.

The response of the majority of commentators has been to play down the miraculous element. Many have suggested that what actually happened was that the crowd, who would surely have brought provisions with them, were reluctant to bring them out for fear of having to share them, but were persuaded by the example of Jesus and the disciples to do just that. Thus according to this school of thought, the feeding of the five thousand is a moral miracle, people overcoming selfishness and agreeing to share what they have got with those who have nothing.

It sounds plausible enough, but once we begin to look at the story through the eyes of the Gospel compilers it loses some of its plausibility.

First of all, this is the only miracle to be included in all four Gospels. That suggests two things—that it made an enormous impact on its eye-witnesses, which was conveyed through the oral tradition to the Gospel writers; and that it had tremendous importance in their understanding of Jesus and his message.

To take the second first, a literal approach to the miracle would not suggest any great depths of doctrine in it. Apart from the obvious conclusions—that Jesus had the power of the Creator to multiply matter, and that he had compassion on those who were physically (and by analogy spiritually) hungry—the literalist will once again read the story, note the power and love of Jesus and move on. That appears to reverence the authority of Scripture, and it shows faith in its reliability, but it falls short of an imaginative grasp of the meaning of the story.

But the sceptics, or naturalists, also seem to fall short of the story's significance. Frankly, the 'sandwich-sharing'

explanation does not do anything like justice to the four
Gospel accounts of the miracle. Why should so comparatively trivial an incident have made such a impression? Is an
exercise in co-operative catering really so earth-shattering
that the report of it should merit inclusion by all four
evangelists? And, more significantly, would it justify John's
reported conversation between Jesus and the Jews, in which
he accuses the multitude of flocking after him because they
had shared in the miraculous feeding of the multitude?[5]
They were hardly likely to be so extravagantly motivated by
an exhibition of sandwich-sharing.

The clue is surely in what the story teaches, and here
John provides the key. His account of the feeding of the
multitude is followed by the discourse on the 'Bread of Life',
culminating in our Lord's claim that his flesh, given for the
life of the world, is that bread of life, and that 'unless you
eat the flesh of the Son of Man and drink his blood you can
have no life in you'.[6]

There can be little doubt what John had in mind here.
His Gospel was a product of the mature reflection of the
Church on the life of Jesus. That Church was one in which
the eucharist was assuming a more and more central and
unitive role—the importance of the rite is already evident in
Acts,[7] and in the earliest Epistles.[8] Naturally the evangelist,
reflecting on Jesus feeding the multitude, saw in it an
inspired prophecy of what the Church experienced every
Sunday. Indeed, in John's account of the miracle the people
ate 'the bread over which the Lord gave thanks'—an action
which is, of course, literally a 'eucharist' in Greek. Jesus
provided for the thousands then; now he provides for the

5 John 6:26
6 John 6:53
7 Acts 2:42; 20:7
8 e.g. 1 Corinthians 10:16,17; 11:23-34

tens of thousands. The bread he gave on the hillside was, in his own words, 'perishable'. The bread he gives now—his own flesh—is the food of eternal life, which satisfies those who eat it, so that they never hunger or thirst again.

So the feeding of the five thousand seemed to each of the Gospel compilers to be a story that was absolutely central to the Church's understanding of the ministry of Jesus. Something happened on that hillside that was extraordinary, memorable and relevant. From the account as we have it it is difficult to work out exactly what it was in terms of actions, but we can see what it was in terms of effect. Jesus fed the multitude, and he still does. It seems impossible to account for the respect and reverence with which this story is retold unless *something* miraculous happened, and unless it had a deep significance for the Church. I am sure both are true, and that the only way to appreciate them to the full is to read the story with faith and imagination.

When we come to the Bible we are, in J. B. Phillips' vivid phrase,[9] like electricians rewiring an old house. Every now and then, when we think we are working on something totally dead, we get a shock and find it is, in fact, still alive. It is the task of every Bible reader, but even more so of every teacher and preacher, to treat it like live material, to welcome the shocks, and to remove the rubbish of centuries that has deadened its effect in the past.

[9] In the Foreword to *Letters to Young Churches* (Bles)

12: POSTSCRIPT

In the course of one week recently I read two statements in the Press which purported to explain why the Church today is largely ineffective, and how it could regain the respect of the uncommitted.

The first, by six clergymen in the *Church Times*, said that the Church had failed because it had failed to proclaim an inerrant Bible, and would only command attention when it did so. The second, in the *Guardian*, gave a rather different picture.

'In Britain,' wrote Trevor Beeson, 'the Christian community as a whole is now faced with two serious challenges. The first concerns the intellectual credibility of the Christian faith itself. While the overwhelming majority of the British people are sensitive to the religious dimension of life, an ever decreasing number of them are able to accept the traditional statements of Christian doctrine . . .'

I had little difficulty in sympathising with both writers. In one sense, and for one section of uncommitted people, the Church would regain respect if it unambiguously proclaimed an infallible message based on an infallible book. There are enough people whose lives are built on sand who are desperate to find absolute security. They are not looking for more and more questions, or a lifelong search, but for answers. For such people, the slogan 'The Bible says . . .' has an immediate appeal.

But as we have seen, the phrase 'The Bible says . . .' begs a lot of questions itself. What *does* the Bible say? To whom is it saying it? What is the context, background and literary form of the passage in question? Is it to be taken literally, or figuratively, or allegorically? After all, 'the Bible says' some very strange things, if they are picked out at random—including the quite unambiguous statement 'There is no God'![1]

At the same time, there is no doubt that Trevor Beeson is right to say that a decreasing number of people find 'the traditional statements of Christian doctrine' credible. For them, simply making the same statements, but more dogmatically, is no answer at all. They know, many of them, what the Bible says, or at any rate what it appears to say, and they simply cannot swallow it. They have good reasons for believing that the world was not created in seven days, that Balaam's ass did not speak to him, that the sun did not orbit backwards and Samson did not annihilate a thousand Philistines with the jawbone of an ass. They are not so sure, but they also suspect that Jesus did not walk on water or turn some rather different water into wine.

In this scepticism they are not simply being perverse, obtuse or arrogant, but, in many cases, honestly trying to follow what their reason demands. They would like to believe—they have a 'sensitivity to the religious dimension of life'—but they cannot over-ride the nagging voice of reason.

Can the Church find a way of giving certainty to those who are looking for it, and at the same time meeting those who, for good and honest reasons, find great difficulty in

[1] Psalm 14:1

accepting the Christian faith as it has traditionally been offered? It is no use offering the first group a vague message devoid of any authority; and no use offering the second group a Bible which they are simply told to accept and believe at face value.

I hope I have begun to show in this book how both groups can be met with the same message. The first group may be reassured that the Bible will convey to them faithfully and without error all the truth that they need to know for salvation. The second group may be reassured that most of the things they have found so incredible in the Bible are peripheral to that truth.

In both cases, something of a revolution is required in their approach to the Bible. Those who want an infallible book will have to accept that only God is infallible, and to work at their reading of the Bible until they discover what he is saying through its human writers. A slogan Christianity, based on 'texts' often torn from their context, is a thing of straw. It will not give them the certainty they need in the face of a cynical, unbelieving world. By all means let us hold firmly to the great traditional doctrines of the faith. They are based on what God has said and the Church has received. But we should not tie them to a crude literalism where the Bible is concerned, or we shall simply and needlessly alienate the other group of people.

Those people—the ones who find traditional Christian doctrine hard to accept—must be shown that in many cases the difficulties they encounter are phantoms created by a crude and faulty approach to the Bible. Time and again I meet intelligent young people, and older ones, for that matter, who were brought up in conservative churches, or belonged to evangelical youth movements or to a college Christian union, but now say they are unable to believe what they were taught. They are not happy or satisfied unbelievers. Very often they report their situation wistfully—'I would like to believe . . . I would love to have a genuine faith to live by'—but they suffer from the delusion that unless they can accept everything in the Bible as literally, historically, scientifically and factually true, then they are 'unbelievers'.

They are, in fact, the innocent victims of the 'plastic balloon' theory of infallibility. The Bible is filled with a certain quantity of 'truth', like a plastic balloon filled with water. If the surface of the balloon is punctured, even by a minute prick, the 'truth' will gradually but inevitably drain away, until nothing is left at all. This 'all or nothing' approach is taught in many churches, youth movements and Christian unions, and many people (including many of the ones who have ceased 'believing') accept it as a reasonable position.

In fact, it is totally unreasonable. There is no balloon. There is no measured quantity of truth. And, most important of all, truth is not like water. It is not all the same, equally important, equally non-negotiable. There are central truths—the incarnation, redemption, judgment—but there are also secondary truths. There is history, allegory, poetry, story. Truth comes in different ways and is believed at different levels. Otherwise, to believe that Jesus is the Son of God, and brings salvation through his death and resurrection, would count for nothing if one disbelieved in Noah's ark; and that is plainly ridiculous.

In any case, as I have tried to argue, to make a particular and faulty interpretation of the Bible into the one acid test of faith is totally wrong. Young people have been stuffed full of nonsense about creation, for instance—that evolution is anti-Christian, or that Adam and Eve, the fruit and the serpent are part of the historical record of the planet. They are even told that God created the earth complete with its fossil record!

Then, when they begin to study science or history seriously, they find that these things are literally incredible. Yet they have been told that to believe them is an integral part of being a Christian. The only course open to them is to accept that they are no longer Christians, and it is a course that many of them take sadly and reluctantly.

But God does not require anyone to believe what is incredible. We gain no merit in his eyes by denying our reason and believing the impossible. His truth, through the incarnation, the Church and the Scriptures, is reasonable, though that is not to say that it can be apprehended by reason alone. Because it deals in the things of the Spirit, it can only be spiritually discerned by faith. But that is not to put faith and reason at loggerheads. God is the author of faith and the creator of reason. Let them work together!

We have a Bible that speaks firmly, faithfully and without error all the truth that God wants us to know for our salvation: so there is assurance, there is confidence. And we have a Bible that is alive and active, not dead and static: so there is no need to be weighed down with the heavy chains of literalism. God has given us truth, freely and generously, minds to understand it and his Spirit to minister it to our spirits.

If we come to the Scriptures with faith and with an imagination fired by the Holy Spirit, it will not be a book of problems, difficulties and contradictions, but a Word of life.

BACKGROUND READING

I have relied heavily for the theological basis of this book on
two sources, both of which I should like to acknowledge,
but neither of which can be held responsible for the views I
have expressed.
Obeying Christ in a Changing World—Chapter 4, 'Understanding God's Word Today' by Tony Thiselton (Fount).
De Divina Revelatione (Divine Revelation)—The Second
Vatican Ecumenical Council (Catholic Truth Society):
especially paragraphs 7, 11, 12, 13, 18 and 19.